R00341 18796

FORM 125 M

EDUCATION & PHILOSOPHY

The Chicago Public Library

Received FEB 2 1984

The Middle Level Principalship

Volume I:

A Survey of Middle Level Principals and Programs

Jerry Valentine
Donald C. Clark
Neal C. Nickerson, Jr.
James W. Keefe

Report of
National Study of Schools in the Middle

National Association of Secondary School Principals
1904 Association Drive • Reston, Virginia 22091

About the authors:

Jerry Valentine is associate professor of educational administration, College of Education, University of Missouri—Columbia.

Donald C. Clark is professor of secondary education, University of Arizona.

Neal C. Nickerson, Jr. is professor of educational administration, University of Minnesota.

James W. Keefe is director of research, National Association of Secondary School Principals.

ISBN 0-88210-132-3
Copyright © 1981
All Rights Reserved
National Association of Secondary School Principals
1904 Association Drive, Reston, Va. 22091

Contents

Tables v
Foreword xi
Introduction xiii
I. Personal and Professional Characteristics of the Middle Level Principal 1
II. Tasks and Problems of the Middle Level Principal 34
III. Staff, Students, and Community 45
IV. School Programs 56
V. Principals View Middle Level Issues 82
VI. Principal and Program Profiles 99
Appendix A: The Questionnaires 111
Appendix B: Supplementary Data 135

**Steering Committee for the
National Study of Schools in the Middle**

    Kenneth M. Brashear
    Will Ella Brown
    Eugene B. Jump
    Tom Maglaras
    Robert Mills
    Donald A. Stokes

Research Team for the Study

    Jerry Valentine, *Chairman*
    Donald C. Clark
    Anthony Gregorc
    James W. Keefe
    Neal C. Nickerson, Jr.

Supported by the Geraldine R. Dodge Foundation

Tables

1. Distribution of Principals by Sex 2
2. Sex by Grade Level 2
3. Sex by Population 3
4. Sex by Per-Pupil Expenditure 3
5. Sex by Enrollment 3
6. Sex by Region 3
7. Distribution of Principals by Age 4
8. Age by Sex 4
9. Age by Grade Level 5
10. Age by Population 5
11. Age by Enrollment 6
12. Ethnic Distribution of Principals 6
13. Ethnicity by Sex 6
14. Ethnicity by Population 7
15. Ethnicity by Per-Pupil Expenditure 7
16. Ethnicity by Geographic Region 7
17. Age at Initial Appointment 8
18. Age at First Principalship by Sex 9
19. Age at First Principalship by Grade Level 9
20. Age at First Principalship by Population 9
21. Age at First Principalship by Enrollment 10
22. Number of Principalships 11
23. Years in the Principalship 11
24. Years in the Principalship by Sex 11
25. Years as Principal in Current School 12
26. Years as Principal in This School by Sex 12
27. Years as Principal in This School by Grade Level 13
28. Years as Principal in This School by Region 13
29. Last Position Prior to Middle Level Principalship 14
30. Position Prior to Principalship by Sex 14
31. Position Prior to Principalship by Grade Level 16
32. Years in Last Position Prior to Middle Level Principalship 16
33. Years in Last Position by Sex 17
34. Years Teaching Prior to Present Position 17
35. Years of Teaching Experience by Sex 17
36. Undergraduate College 18
37. Major Field of Undergraduate Study 18
38. Undergraduate Major by Grade Level 20

39	Major Field of Graduate Study	20
40	Highest Degree Earned	21
41	Highest Earned Degree by Sex	21
42	Highest Earned Degree by Grade Level	22
43	Highest Earned Degree by Enrollment	22
44	Administrative Certification	22
45	Administrative Certification by Sex	23
46	Administrative Certification by Grade Level	23
47	Administrative Certification by Enrollment	24
48	Current Annual Salary	25
49	Salary by Sex	26
50	Salary Based upon Community Population	26
51	Salary by Per-Pupil Expenditure	26
52	Basis for Salary Determination by Population	27
53	Length of Salary Contract	28
54	Tenure as a Principal	28
55	Tenure by Sex	28
56	Tenure by Grade Level	28
57	Tenure by Region	29
58	Participation in Professional Activities	29
59	Participation in Higher Education Studies by Sex	29
60	Participation in Activities of Professional Associations by Highest Degree	30
61	Number of Civic and Political Organization Memberships	30
62	Principal's Career Aspirations	31
63	Principal's Career Aspirations by Sex	31
64	Principal's Career Aspirations by Grade Level	32
65	Commitment to Same Career Choice	32
66	Commitment to Same Career Choice by Sex	32
67	Average Work Week of Principals	34
68	Average Work Week by Sex	34
69	Rank Order of Time Allocation for a Typical Work Week	35
70	Teaching Responsibilities	37
71	Principal's Rating of Job Characteristics	38
72	Actual Prestige of Position by Sex	38
73	Self-Fulfillment Based upon Salary	39
74	Self-Fulfillment Based upon Grade Level	39
75	Self-Fulfillment Based upon Same Career Choice	39
76	Authority in Staffing Practices	40
77	Authority in Staffing Practices by Self-Fulfillment	40
78	Authority To Fill Teacher Vacancies	40
79	Participation in Budget Allocation for School	41

80	Participation in Budget Allocation by Population	41
81	Authority in Allocation of Discretionary Funds	42
82	Authority in Allocation of Discretionary Funds by Self-Fulfillment	42
83	Administrative Roadblocks	43
84	School Staff Availability	45
85	School Staff by Community Population	46
86	Ratio of Female Teachers by Grade Level	47
87	Teacher Preparation for Middle Level	47
88	Forms of Teacher Preparation	47
89	Teacher-Pupil Ratio by Enrollment	49
90	Teacher-Pupil Ratio by Per-Pupil Expenditure	49
91	Enrollment Based upon Grade Level Configuration	49
92	Average Daily Attendance by Grade Level	50
93	Average Daily Attendance by Enrollment	50
94	Number of Schools by Community Population	51
95	Number of Schools by Geographic Region	51
96	Parent Involvement by Community Population	52
97	Parent Involvement by Geographic Region	53
98	Parent/Citizen Involvement in School Operation by Grade Level	53
99	Parent Involvement in Planning/Advisory Capacity by Grade Level	53
100	Community Pressure Groups by Population	54
101	Grade Level by Type of School	56
102	Type of School by Enrollment	57
103	Grade Level Across Regions	57
104	Grade Level Within Regions	58
105	Years Using the Current Organizational Pattern by Grade Level	58
106	Reasons for Change to 5-6-7-8 or 6-7-8 Configurations	59
107	Average Per-Pupil Expenditure by Grade Level	61
108	Types of Facilities by Grade Level	61
109	Comparison of Types of Facilities	62
110	Instructional Organization by Grade Level	63
111	Subject Organization for Instruction	64
112	Required Courses and Electives	65
113	Types of Programs for Which Students May Enroll by Grade Level Organization	66
114	Types of Programs for Which Students May Enroll by Population	66
115	Types of Programs for Which Students May Enroll by Enrollment	67
116	Ability Grouping by Grade Level Organization	67

117	Criteria for Grouping Students by Grade Level Organization	69
118	Scope of Ability Grouping by Grade Level Organization	69
119	Comparison of Grouping Policies: NASSP 1980 and NASSP 1966	70
120	Gifted Programs by Grade Level Organization	71
121	Criteria for Admittance to Gifted Programs by Enrollment	71
122	Criteria for Admittance to Gifted Programs by Grade Level Organization	72
123	Organizational Format for Gifted Programs by Grade Level Organization	72
124	Organizational Format for Gifted Programs by Per-Pupil Expenditure	74
125	Funded Programs by Grade Level Organization	75
126	Interscholastic Sports for Boys	76
127	Interscholastic Sports for Girls	76
128	Extracurricular Activities by Grade Level Organization	77
129	Articulation Problems by Grade Level Organization	78
130	Regional Accreditation by Grade Level Organization	78
131	Parent Conferences	79
132	Data Processing by Grade Level	79
133	Tasks of American Schools	83
134	Opinions About Ability Grouping Policies by Grade Level Organization	84
135	Comparisons of NASSP 1980 and NASSP 1966 Studies on Current Ability Grouping Policy and Principal Opinion About Ability Grouping Policies	85
136	Opinions About Individualized Promotion by Grade Level Organization	86
137	Opinions About Individualized Promotion by Enrollment	86
138	Opinions About Competency Testing for Promotion by Grade Level	86
139	Opinions About Competency Testing for Promotion by Enrollment	86
140	Opinions Whether Interscholastic Sports Should Be Provided at the Middle Level	87
141	Opinions About What Interscholastic Sports Should Be Provided at the Middle Level	88
142	Opinions About the Ideal Grade Organizational Structure for a Middle Level School	89

143	Opinions About the Ideal Middle Level Grade Organizational Structure by Region	89
144	Comparisons of 1980 and 1966 NASSP Studies: Ideal Grade Level Organizational Structure	89
145	Opinions About Optimal Number of Students for a Middle Level School by Grade Level Organization	90
146	Opinions About Optimal Number of Students for a Middle Level School by Enrollment	91
147	Personal Characteristics of Teachers and Their Importance to Successful Teaching	92
148	Professional Characteristics of Teachers and Their Importance to Successful Teaching	93
149	Ranking of Special Preservice Middle Level Courses	94
150	Ranking of Special Preservice Middle Level Courses— NASSP 1980 and NASSP 1966	95
151	Opinions Regarding Support for Administrative Tenure by Region	96

Foreword

The National Association of Secondary School Principals (NASSP) is committed to the study of secondary school principals and programs on a systematic basis. This commitment extends to all of the transitional levels of secondary education, including "schools in the middle"—intermediate, middle, and junior high schools.

This publication is the first of two volumes on the National Study of Schools in the Middle. It reports survey data from a national sample of 1,413 middle level principals on the personal and professional traits of principals, their job tasks and problems, on student, staff, and community characteristics, on school programs, and on selected educational issues. Summary profiles of principals and programs will be found in Chapter VI along with notable findings and conclusions. This volume does not include all the information gathered from principals' responses to the survey questionnaires, but data tapes are available to researchers and other persons or organizations interested in the comprehensive file.

The NASSP is grateful to the Steering Committee and the Research Team for their time and talent. Special thanks go to Jerry Valentine for his dedicated and creative leadership of the national research team. The study could not have been completed, of course, without the generous cooperation of the principals and their schools.

Contemporary research stresses the importance of the principal to effective schooling and emphasizes the focal position of the principal as planner, leader, facilitator, and decision maker for the school. At the same time, other studies, including the 1978 NASSP survey of *The Senior High School Principalship*, document a continuing need to redefine the principalship. This study should contribute much to a heightened perception of the principalship and school programs at the middle level. It is the most comprehensive look at this important level of education since the 1966 NASSP *Report of the Junior High-School Principalship*.

James W. Keefe
Director of Research
NASSP

Introduction

Many educators in America believe that middle level education has progressed through an interesting and significant period in the past decade. Some would say that we have witnessed a "rebirth" of interest in the middle level—a rebirth that has been healthy for educators, for communities, and most importantly, for students.

Numerous issues have arisen in the minds of middle level educators and have appeared in the literature on the middle level.

- Is the junior high or the middle school the most appropriate organizational delivery system for the middle level student?
- Are middle schools significantly different from junior high schools in program content and instructional delivery?
- Has the middle school established itself as a unique level of education?
- Does the junior high or the middle school best meet the needs of today's students?

These and other concerns have stimulated middle level educators to reassess programs, with renewed emphasis on the importance of the individual student. The roles, functions, and skills of administrators and teachers and the programs they implement are now, probably more than ever before, being scrutinized and questioned. Educators are looking at the community, the parents, the skills of the staff, and the students themselves before determining which programs are appropriate. And just as certainly as needs and expectations vary from community to community, so will specific middle level programs vary from one community to another.

What then are the programs currently employed in middle level education throughout the United States? What are the skills and backgrounds of the teachers implementing these programs? And, of most interest in this study, what are the skills, functions, and roles of the middle level administrator charged with providing leadership for these schools?

The National Association of Secondary School Principals, with support from the Geraldine R. Dodge Foundation, proposed to answer these and other similar questions through a national study of schools in the middle. The specific purposes of the study were to:

1. develop a base of knowledge about the middle level principalship including personal characteristics, professional objectives, and job-related tasks and expectations;

2. describe similarities and differences of the middle level principalship considering the grade levels administered as well as other demographic data;
3. develop a base of knowledge about middle level educational programs, organizational structures, instructional practices, and decision making;
4. describe similarities and differences of middle level programs based on grade level organization as well as other demographic data about the community and population served;
5. describe programmatic and administrative characteristics in schools administered by principals designated as "successful or effective";
6. extrapolate future trends in middle level education and the middle level principalship.

The study was implemented in two major phases. This report, *A Survey of Middle Level Principals and Programs*, represents Phase I and presents survey questionnaire data collected during 1980. Phase II will be reported in a second volume entitled *The Effective Middle Level Principal*.

INSTRUMENTATION

The first draft of survey questions for collecting Phase I data was developed by the study research team. The revised questions were based upon suggestions of the NASSP Committee on Middle Level Education and the study Steering Committee. Ninety-six items were identified as appropriate measures of the five themes to be studied. The themes were:

1. Personal and Professional Characteristics of the Middle Level Principal.
2. Tasks and Problems of the Middle Level Principal.
3. Staff, Students, and Community.
4. School Programs.
5. Principals View Middle Level Issues.

The instrument was field-tested early in 1980 and data were collected in the spring of the same year.

In 1965, NASSP sponsored a national survey of junior high school principals from which numerous items were included in the present study for the purpose of update. A national study of middle schools conducted by Brooks in 1977 provided some help in designing the instrument. Key questions from NASSP's 1978 study of *The Senior*

High School Principalship also were included for cross-comparison purposes.

The present study furnishes an opportunity for historical perspective and, for the first time in a study of national scope, a detailed look at the entire middle level, both the principalship and the program. The normative-descriptive-comparative data of the study provide a basis for: understanding the current state-of-the-art in middle level education; identifying middle level changes, or lack thereof, during the past 15 years; and interpreting the significance of Phase II findings, an in-depth study of effective principals.

SAMPLE

A random sample of 2,600 middle level schools was identified as the survey population. This sample represents more than 20 percent of the some 12,000 middle level schools in the United States.

Two forms of the survey questionnaire were developed to permit a wide range of questions while limiting the time needed for completion. Each form (A or B) was mailed to a different group of 1,300 principals. From the sample, 1,413 principals returned usable questionnaires, a 54 percent rate of return. This rate was considered acceptable because it represented data from more than 10 percent of middle level schools in the country.

Moreover, analysis of selected demographic items from the first and the last 100 returns showed no statistically significant differences. Late respondents are typically similar to nonrespondents and can be thought of as representative of them.

The average time required for each principal to complete the survey was somewhat longer than one hour.

DESCRIPTION OF THE SAMPLE

The 1,413 principals and schools in the study represent a broad cross section of the grade combinations of middle level education. For the purposes of the study, a middle level school was described as one encompassing any grade or grade combinations from grades 5 through 9. Each questionnaire required the principal to identify the grade levels of the school. Data presented in the study will frequently reflect these grade combinations so that educators can study the relationship of the issues to the configurations. Of the schools surveyed, 42 percent included grades 7-8-9, 31 percent grades 7-8, 15 percent grades 6-7-8, 4 percent grades 5-6-7-8, and 8 percent other grades or combinations. This distribution varies up to 10 percent from the Market Data Retrieval (Westport, Conn.), resource file from which it was drawn.

The schools in the study were representative of each of the geographic regions of the country. Eight percent came from the New

England states, 15 percent from the Middle Atlantic, 18 percent from the South, 33 percent from the Midwest, 5 percent from the Rocky Mountains, 9 percent from the Southwest, and 12 percent from the Far West, including Alaska and Hawaii.

Community population was an important variable considered. Large cities of 150,000 or more persons represented 13 percent of the schools in the study and related suburban schools represented 21 percent. Twenty-three percent of the schools reflected cities of 25,000 to 149,000, 22 percent communities of 5,000 to 24,999, and 21 percent schools in rural communities.

Each principal was asked to indicate school size (enrollment). Of the schools represented in this study, 20 percent had fewer than 400 students, 25 percent enrolled 400 to 599 students, 24 percent 600-799, 18 percent 800-999, 10 percent 1,000-1,399, and 3 percent 1,400 or more students.

Exclusive of capital outlay, 38 percent of the schools had a per-pupil expenditure of less than $1,200, 43 percent expended between $1,200 and $1,799, and 19 percent spent $1,800 or more.

The demographic data reflect the representativeness of the sample and provide a basis for analyzing responses by school characteristics throughout the study.

ORGANIZATION OF THE REPORT

This report is not simply an item-by-item list of responses to the 96 survey questions. Relationships between questions are discussed, particularly as those relationships reflect common themes. Data are analyzed with respect to demographic characteristics.

The chapters of the report are organized thematically to describe: 1. personal and professional characteristics of the principal, 2. tasks and problems of the principal, 3. staff, students, and community, 4. school programs, and 5. principals' views of middle level issues. Data reported in these chapters provide a frame of reference for viewing the contemporary middle level principalship and middle level programs. These data, in turn, can serve as benchmarks for subsequent studies of middle level education in the 1980s and beyond.

The Steering Committee and the Research Team believe that the principal is the key person in the development of a dynamic educational program. From this study, middle level principals can develop a better understanding of the current status of their principalship and middle level education, identify areas of concern that should be addressed at the local, state, or national levels, and pursue these concerns with the conviction that providing educational opportunities for all students is an appropriate and approachable goal.

I. Personal and Professional Characteristics of the Middle Level Principal

The National Association of Secondary School Principals first studied the junior high school principalship in 1966. That study provided descriptive data about some 7,000 principals. It attempted to discover what kind of people junior high school principals were and what they did. It provided baseline data for a continuing history and analysis of middle level education.

The present study is an expanded look at junior high, intermediate, and middle level schools—the entire middle level—with an eye to providing current information about the middle level principalship and its tasks. Certainly the role has changed since 1966.

The first section of this report provides information about those changes. It brings up to date the factual information necessary for a critical evaluation of the professional role of the middle level principal. Several questions are answered. The most basic one asks, "What are the characteristics of the 1980 middle level principal?" Both personal and professional data are supplied.

Other questions deal with comparisons over time, and between middle level principals and other principals.

- How do present middle level principals differ from junior high principals as described in the 1966 NASSP Junior High study?
- How do they differ from senior high principals as pictured in the 1965 and 1978 NASSP studies?
- How do they differ from elementary principals as reported in the 1968 and 1979 studies by the National Association of Elementary School Principals (NAESP)?

Comparable data are not available from all studies on all factors, but where comparisons can be made, they are reported.

THE TYPICAL PRINCIPAL

The typical principal of the contemporary school in the middle is a white male, age 45 to 54, with a master of arts degree in secondary school administration plus some additional graduate credits, who moved to the principalship from an assistant principalship. The typical principal is slightly older than his/her 1966 counterpart and has more advanced training and experience. The teaching field typically is social studies (at both points in time). There is a greater likelihood that the principal is female than in 1966.

PERSONAL FACTORS

Sex Distribution of Principals

The percentage of middle level principals who are female has increased since 1966. The reverse is true for both senior high and elementary school principals during the same time period.

Table 1 of this 1980 study shows that 6 percent of the middle level respondents were female. In 1966, the figure was 4 percent. This increase runs contrary to the decline in the number of female principals at the senior high school—only 7 percent of the 1978 respondents were female, down from 10 percent in the 1965 study. At the elementary level, the percentage of female principals decreased from 22 percent in 1968 to 18 percent in 1979.

Table 2 reveals that only 5 percent of the principals in grade 7-8-9 schools are female. The highest percentage was found in schools encompassing grades 5-6-7-8 where the figure was 9 percent. The presence of lower grades appears to correlate positively with an increase in the number of female principals.

The data in Table 3 indicate that a higher percentage of women (11 percent) serve as middle level principals in large cities than in other population categories. In addition, Tables 4 and 5 establish that a higher

TABLE 1
Distribution of Principals by Sex

Sex	Middle Level 1980	Junior High 1966	Senior High 1978	Senior High 1965	Elementary 1979	Elementary 1968
Male	94	96	93	89	82	78
Female	6	4	7	10	18	22

*All tables represent percentages unless otherwise noted.

TABLE 2
Sex by Grade Level

	1980 Total	7-8-9	7-8	6-7-8	5-6-7-8	Other
Male	94	95	92	92	91	96
Female	6	5	8	8	9	4

TABLE 3
Sex by Population

	1980 Total	City of 150,000+	Suburban	25,000-149,999	5,000-24,999	Rural
Male	94	89	94	93	96	94
Female	6	11	6	7	4	6

TABLE 4
Sex by Per-Pupil Expenditure

	1980 Total	<$1,200	$1,200-1,799	$1,799+
Male	94	88	97	96
Female	6	12	3	4

than average percentage of women are found in districts where the per-pupil expenditure is $1,200 or less (12 percent) and in large schools of 1,400 or more enrollment (9 percent).

Table 6 shows that 13 percent of the Far West respondents were female, the highest percentage reported by any geographic region of the country. The Midwest had the smallest number of female middle level principals, only 3 percent.

Overall, the data indicate a higher percentage of female principals in the following categories:

- in grade level configurations that do not include the ninth grade;
- in cities of 150,000 population or more;
- in districts where the per-pupil expenditure is $1,200 or less;

TABLE 5
Sex by Enrollment

	1980 Total	<400	400-599	600-799	800-999	1,000-1,399	1,400+
Male	94	93	94	93	95	95	91
Female	6	7	6	7	5	5	9

TABLE 6
Sex by Region

	1980 Total	New England	Middle Atlantic	South	Midwest	Southwest	Rocky Mountain	Far West
Male	94	93	94	91	97	93	96	87
Female	6	7	6	9	3	7	4	13

- in schools of 1,400 or more students;
- in the Far West region.

It is not surprising that the number of female, middle level principals has increased since the 1966 study considering the contemporary push for equality of opportunity. It is surprising, however, that this positive growth does not also appear at the elementary or senior high school level.

Age Distribution of Principals

Middle level principals of 1980 appear to be slightly older than their 1966 counterparts. The percentage of principals in the 45-54 age brackets increased from 31 percent to 42 percent. This increased age is also true for senior high principals. The increase may reflect not only retrenchment in the job market but more demanding requirements for principal certification in many states (see Table 7).

Slight differences in age between the sexes can be seen in Table 8. Whereas 57 percent of the males were 45 or older, 61 percent of the females were in that age category. Table 9 indicates younger principals

TABLE 7
Distribution of Principals by Age

	Middle Level 1980	Junior High 1966	Senior High 1978	Senior High 1965	Elementary 1979	Brooks 1978
9 or younger	1	2	1	4	2	6
30-34	8	8	8	12	12	11
35-39	15	19	16	18	15	17
40-44	18	18	22	16	17	23
45-49	21	15	22	15	20	25
50-54	21	16	19	15	19	
55-59	11	14	8	12	11	18
60+	5	8	5	8	6	

TABLE 8
Age by Sex

	1980 Total	Male	Female
29 or younger	1	1	1
30-34	8	9	7
35-39	15	15	19
40-44	18	18	12
45-49	21	21	24
50-54	21	21	24
55-59	11	11	7
60+	5	4	6

TABLE 9
Age by Grade Level

	1980 Total	7-8-9	7-8	6-7-8	5-6-7-8	Other
29 or younger	1	1	1	1	7	1
30-34	8	7	9	12	6	8
35-39	15	12	16	16	23	21
40-44	18	19	17	16	27	23
45-49	21	21	23	17	14	19
50-54	21	23	20	24	18	15
55-59	11	13	11	9	5	7
60+	5	5	3	5	0	6

TABLE 10
Age by Population

	1980 Total	City of 150,000+	Suburban	25,000-149,999	5,000-24,999	Rural
29 or younger	1	1	0	1	1	2
30-34	8	5	7	4	11	16
35-39	15	7	14	13	17	20
40-44	18	11	19	17	16	23
45-49	21	29	22	19	21	15
50-54	21	23	25	29	16	14
55-59	11	16	9	12	13	8
60+	5	8	4	5	5	2

were to be found in schools with younger children. In 7-8-9 schools, 20 percent of the principals were 39 or younger. In 6-7-8 schools, that figure jumped to 29 percent and in 5-6-7-8 schools, to 36 percent.

There is a negative correlation between community size and the age of the principal (Table 10). Only 13 percent of the principals in the largest cities were age 39 or younger. In the suburbs it was 21 percent; in the smaller cities, 29 percent; and in rural areas the percentage was 39 percent. Table 11 represents the relationship between school size and the age of the principal. In the largest category, 1,400 or more students, only 16 percent of the principals were 39 or younger.

Generally, middle level principals are older in schools that include the ninth grade, are found in large cities, and have 1,000 or more pupils.

Probably the size-to-age relationship is a result both of experience and stability. There is less movement of individuals out of large districts than small ones. Teachers and principals typically move from a smaller district to a larger one, and remain there. This progression may account for a somewhat older age in the largest categories at the time of the initial principalship.

TABLE 11
Age by Enrollment

	1980 Total	<400	400-599	600-799	800-999	1,000-1,399	1,400+
29 or younger	1	4	1	1	0	0	0
30-34	8	16	9	8	7	1	0
35-39	15	21	15	13	13	10	16
40-44	18	19	19	18	15	15	12
45-49	21	12	22	22	20	30	10
50-54	21	14	19	23	29	25	35
55-59	11	7	10	12	14	14	20
60+	5	7	5	4	4	5	7

Ethnicity of Principals

At the middle level only 8 percent of the respondents identified themselves as other than white. At the senior high level only 4 percent were so identified. The 1979 elementary school principal study showed that more than 9 percent were other than white. Table 12 contains these comparative data.

More females than males were reported as nonwhite. Table 13 shows that 12 percent of the females were black; 2 percent Chicano/Hispanic; 2 percent American Indian; and 1 percent Asian—a total of 17 percent nonwhite. Only 8 percent of the males were nonwhite.

TABLE 12
Ethnic Distribution of Principals

Ethnicity	Middle Level 1980	Senior High 1978	Elementary 1979
White	92	96	90.7
Black	6	3	5.5
Chicano/Hispanic	1	0.6	0.9
American Indian	0.4	0.2	2.3
Asian	0.1	0.2 }	0.6
Other	0.5	0	

TABLE 13
Ethnicity by Sex

	1980 Total	Male	Female
White	92	92	83
Black	6	6	12
Chicano/Hispanic	1	1	2
American Indian	<1	<1	2
Asian	<1	<1	1
Other	<1	<1	0

No major differences in ethnicity were reported by age or grade levels in the school enrollment. Table 14 shows, however, that 19 percent of the principals in large cities were nonwhite. Only 4 percent in smaller cities and 6 percent in rural areas fell into that category. Table 15 reveals that in those districts spending $1,200 or less per pupil, 16 percent of the principals were nonwhite. In the high expenditure districts, the figure was only 2 percent. The South has the highest percentage of nonwhite middle level principals. Table 16 shows it to be 23 percent. The Far West has the highest number of Asian principals—8 percent.

TABLE 14
Ethnicity by Population

	1980 Total	City of 150,000+	Suburban	25,000-149,999	5,000-24,999	Rural
White	92	81	94	90	96	94
Black	6	18	3	7	3	5
Chicano/Hispanic	1	1	1	2	0	1
American Indian	<1	0	1	<1	<1	<1
Asian	<1	<1	<1	0	0	0
Other	<1	0	1	1	1	<1

TABLE 15
Ethnicity by Per-Pupil Expenditure

	1980 Total	<$1,200	$1,200-1,799	$1,800+
White	92	84	94	98
Black	6	11	3	2
Chicano/Hispanic	1	2	1	0
American Indian	<1	1	1	0
Asian	<1	1	0	0
Other	<1	1	1	0

TABLE 16
Ethnicity by Geographic Region

	New England	Middle Atlantic	South	Midwest	Southwest	Rocky Mountain	Far West
White	97	95	77	96	92	96	87
Black	2	5	22	3	0	1	2
Chicano/Hispanic	0	0	1	<1	5	3	1
American Indian	0	0	0	<1	1	0	1
Asian	0	0	0	0	0	0	8
Other	1	0	0	<1	1	0	1

A higher than average percentage of nonwhites is found in the following categories:

- female principals
- large cities
- schools having per-pupil expenditure of $1,200 or less
- the South and Far West.

The highest number of nonwhite principals appear to be found in areas and among populations with the largest number of nonwhite students.

PROFESSIONAL FACTORS

Age at Appointment to First Principalship

Respondents were asked to identify their age when they first entered the principalship. Table 17 indicates that 50 percent of the principals were 34 or younger. The 1978 Senior High Principalship study showed the same percentage. At the elementary school level, the figure was 58.5 percent. No comparable data are available from any of the earlier studies. It would appear that principals are appointed to the first principalship at a somewhat younger age at the elementary school level than at the middle or senior high levels.

Females enter the middle level principalship at an older age. Table 18 shows that only 35 percent were 34 or younger at their first principalship. There is a difference in this entering age according to the grade level configuration of the school. Table 19 shows that whereas 44 percent of the principals of 7-8-9 schools were 34 or younger at their first principalship, 67 percent of those in 5-6-7-8 schools fell into that category.

The entering age for principals is younger in rural schools than in other population categories—66 percent enter at age 34 or younger. Table 20 outlines the age by population relationship. This table points

TABLE 17
Age at Initial Appointment

Age	Middle Level 1980	Senior High 1978	Elementary 1979
29 or younger	19	22	58.5
30-34	31	28	
35-39	22	24	38.3
40-44	18	15	
45-49	6	7	
50-54	3	3	3.2
55+	1	0	

TABLE 18
Age at First Principalship by Sex

	1980 Total	Male	Female
29 or younger	19	20	7
30-34	31	32	28
35-39	22	23	16
40-44	18	17	30
45-49	6	6	5
50-54	3	2	12
55+	1	0	2

TABLE 19
Age at First Principalship by Grade Level

	1980 Total	7-8-9	7-8	6-7-8	5-6-7-8	Other
29 or younger	19	16	20	18	29	39
30-34	31	28	35	32	38	25
35-39	22	21	22	25	14	19
40-44	18	23	15	14	14	9
45-49	6	8	4	8	5	4
50-54	3	4	3	3	0	4
55+	1	<1	1	0	0	0

TABLE 20
Age at First Principalship by Population

	1980 Total	City of 150,000+	Suburban	25,000-149,999	5,000-24,999	Rural
29 or younger	19	9	17	14	22	30
30-34	31	23	31	30	35	36
35-39	22	23	26	21	20	18
40-44	18	25	16	24	14	11
45-49	6	12	6	8	5	4
50-54	3	6	3	3	4	1
55+	1	2	1	0	0	0

up that only 32 percent of the principals in the largest cities were 34 or younger upon assuming the principalship. Table 21 shows a similar relationship between age at the first principalship and size of school. It appears that the smaller the school, the younger the beginning age. In schools of 400 or fewer, 69 percent of the principals started at age 34 or younger. In the largest category, 1,400 or more, 25 percent were in that age bracket. Only in schools of 1,000-1,399 was there a smaller figure (23 percent).

TABLE 21
Age at First Principalship by Enrollment

	1980 Total	<400	400-599	600-799	800-999	1,000-1,399	1,400+
29 or younger	19	33	19	20	12	4	0
30-34	31	36	36	28	30	19	25
35-39	22	11	20	23	25	37	42
40-44	18	10	16	20	18	27	17
45-49	6	6	6	5	8	8	8
50-54	3	4	2	3	6	3	8
55+	1	0	1	1	1	2	0

The middle level survey data on age at the first principalship indicate that:

- males attain their first principalship at a younger age than females;
- those beginning in grade 7-8-9 schools are older;
- rural and small town principalships are attained at a younger age than other population categories;
- those beginning in smaller schools are younger.

These data correlate positively with other age factors in the study. Young teachers and principals typically move from small schools and districts to larger ones; thus, they are older when they attain an administrative position in a large city or school. The traditional disregard toward females seeking administrative positions probably accounts for their older age at initial appointment. Women principals likely have come from the ranks of the mature and experienced assistant principals and teachers.

Number of Principalships

Respondents were asked to indicate the number of principalships they have held, including their present position. Table 22 shows that half were still in their first principalship, a figure comparable to the 1978 Senior High School Principalship data. It would be instructive to collect and analyze data on *length* of stay in multiple principalships, especially since discussion about the increasing rate of "principal turnover" is popular today. There may be some significant differences depending on the organizational level (cf. Table 25 discussion for further comment).

Years in the Principalship

No dramatic differences or changes were apparent among the levels in total years in the principalship. Table 23 shows that only 7

TABLE 22
Number of Principalships

Number	Middle Level 1980	Senior High 1978
1	50	49
2	28	29
3	13	15
4	5	5
5	2	2
6	1	1
7	1	0
8	1	0

TABLE 23
Years in the Principalship

Years	Middle Level 1980	Junior High 1966	Senior High 1978	Senior High 1965	Elementary 1979	Elementary 1968	Brooks 1978
1	7	6	5	8	15.4	22.3	15
2-3	12	14	14	14			
4-5	10	14	16	13			
6-7	13	11	12	11	33.8	30.1	34
8-9	11	11	11	10			
10-14	22	18	21	18	37.7	31.6	
15-19	13	11	11	10			51
20-24	8	6	6	6	13.2	16.2	
25+	4	9	4	9			

percent of the middle level principals were in their first *year* at that position. Fifty-three percent have been principals 1-9 years. The 1966 Junior High study showed 56 percent in that range and the 1978 Senior High study, 58 percent.

Females have had less cumulative experience in the principalship than males. Table 24 shows that 76 percent of the women had 1-9 years

TABLE 24
Years in the Principalship by Sex

Years	1980 Total	Male	Female
1	7	7	14
2-3	12	11	19
4-5	10	9	17
6-7	13	13	17
8-9	11	11	9
10-14	22	22	17
15-19	13	14	3
20-24	8	9	3
25+	4	4	1

experience compared to 51 percent for men. This is not unexpected in light of the earlier data on age and sex.

Years as Principal in Current School

Longevity differences in current position are apparent among middle level, senior high, and elementary principals only with the most experienced. Approximately one-third of all principals are in the first 3 years at their present assignment (Table 25). Elementary and middle level principals seem to remain in their positions longer than their senior high colleagues. Twenty-three percent of elementary principals show an incumbency of 12 years or more compared to 19 percent and 12 percent respectively for middle and senior high administrators.

Table 26 indicates that 65 percent of the females have been principals in their current school for three years or less compared to 33 percent for males. These figures parallel previous data on age and experience for females. Women are newer to the middle level principalship.

Schools with grades 5-6-7-8 had the lowest percentage of highly experienced principals of any grade level grouping. Table 27 shows 43 percent of the respondents with three years or less experience in 5-6-7-8 schools. This grade level organization is one of the most recent at the

TABLE 25
Years as Principal in Current School

Years	Middle Level 1980	Junior High 1966	Senior High 1978	Senior High 1965	Elementary 1979	Elementary 1968
1	13	13	12	16		
2	12	14	13	14	34.1	37.6
3	9	12	11	12		
4-5	16	20	19	18		
6-8	19	18	21	15	42.7	32.4
9-11	12	11	11	9		
12-14	8	4	6	5		
15-17	6	3	6	11	23.2	30.0
18+	5	5				

TABLE 26
Years as Principal in This School by Sex

Years	1980 Total	Male	Female
<3	34	33	65
<5	50	48	88
6+	50	52	12

TABLE 27
Years as Principal in This School by Grade Level

Years	1980 Total	7-8-9	7-8	6-7-8	5-6-7-8	Other
1	13	13	14	7	33	12
2	12	15	13	6	10	7
3	9	10	11	10	0	10
4-5	16	14	14	20	29	17
6-8	19	20	20	21	14	6
9-11	12	9	10	16	14	32
12-14	8	10	6	10	0	1
15-17	6	6	6	4	0	11
18+	5	3	6	6	0	4

TABLE 28
Years as Principal in This School by Region

Years	1980 Total	New England	Middle Atlantic	South	Midwest	Southwest	Rocky Mountain	Far West
1	13	13	12	11	11	14	16	60
2	12	8	11	11	15	8	16	7
3	9	13	4	13	7	18	7	6
4-5	16	11	15	19	13	24	13	10
6-8	19	17	24	18	19	13	23	8
9-11	12	24	11	15	10	10	6	1
12-14	8	6	15	5	9	5	6	4
15-17	6	6	6	4	8	3	10	3
18+	5	2	2	4	8	5	3	1

middle level and the relatively short tenure of its administrators likely reflects that fact.

Table 28 reveals that the Far West region had by far the highest percentage of principals reporting three or less years of experience in the current school. Seventy-three percent report that figure compared with no more than 40 percent in any other region. This phenomenon may reflect school district reorganization in the face of declining enrollments.

Tables 25-28, "Years as Principal in This School," show that respondents in the following categories had fewer years in their present principalship than the total sample:

- females
- those in schools of 5-6-7-8
- those in the Far West.

The data do not suggest a turnover rate in the middle level principalship any greater than at the time of the 1966 study. Newness to the principalship is more prevalent in areas with population increases and where there are new schools.

Last Position Prior to Middle Level Principalship

The data in Table 29 indicate that almost half of the respondents moved to the middle level principalship from the assistant principalship. In recent years this has become the typical career move. It is also common for administrators to move from an assistant principalship in a small school or district to the principalship in a larger school or district. Only 12 percent reported moving directly from a position as a middle level teacher to the principalship. Table 30 shows that more females than males—23 percent to 10 percent—attained the principalship from positions other than teacher, assistant principal, or principal. No female came to the middle level principalship from a senior high position. Fifty-one percent of the males compared to only 33 percent of the females came from the assistant principalship.

In schools with grades 5-6-7-8, 33 percent of the principals came directly from a teaching position. None, as Table 31 shows, were

TABLE 29
Last Position Prior to Middle Level Principalship

	Middle Level 1980	Junior High 1966
Elementary teacher	2	18
Middle level teacher	12	
High school teacher	8	13
Assistant principal of an elementary school	2	1
Assistant principal of a middle level school	29	20
Assistant principal of a high school	18	11
Principal of an elementary school	7	6
Principal of a high school	12	6
Guidance counselor	2	
Central office administrator	3	10
Other	5	

TABLE 30
Position Prior to Principalship by Sex

	1980 Total	Male	Female
Teacher	22	21	25
Assistant principal	49	51	33
High school principal	7	7	0
Elementary principal	12	11	19
Other	10	10	23

FIGURE A (Based on Table 31)
Position Prior to Principalship by Grade Level

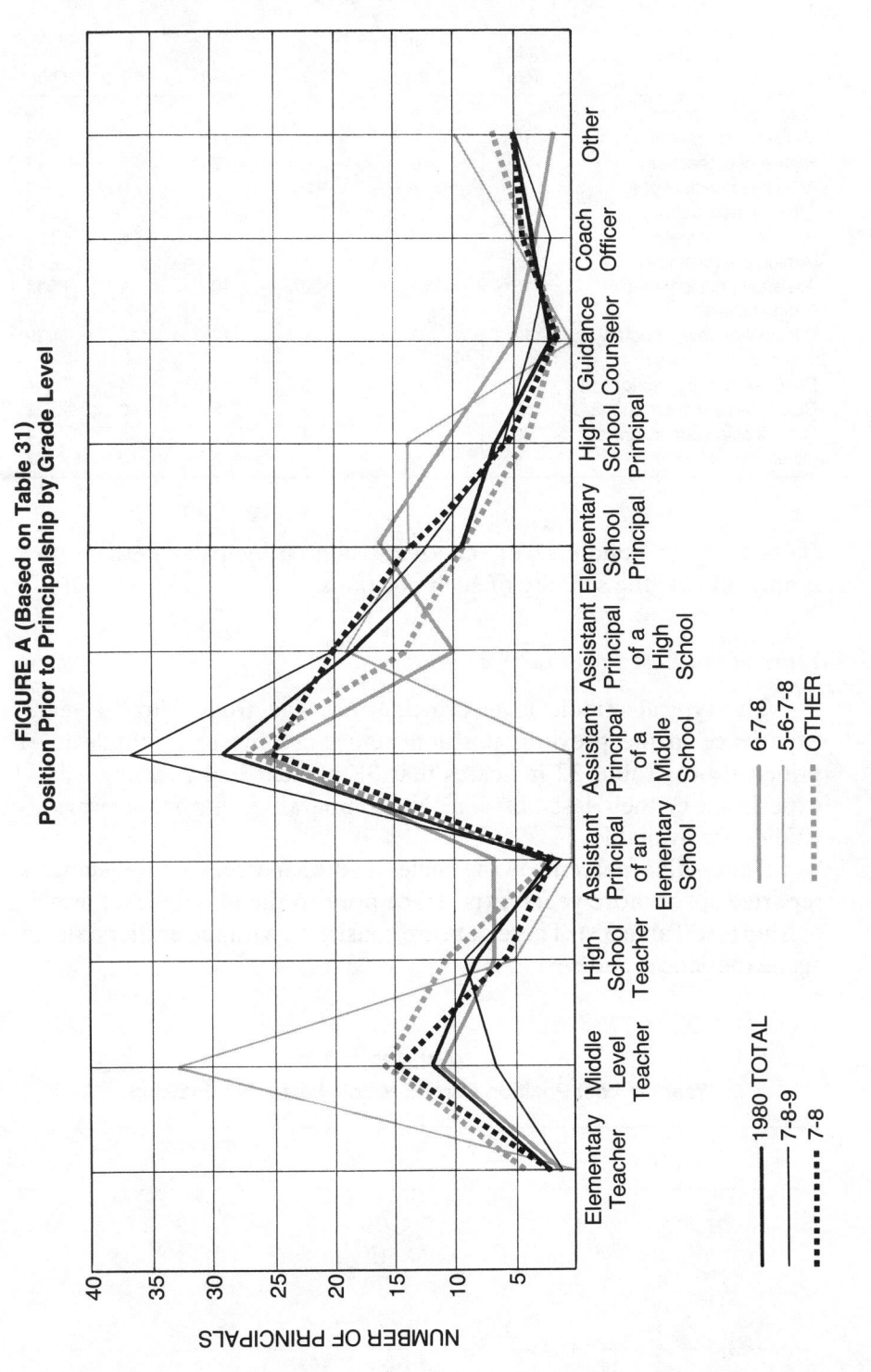

TABLE 31
Position Prior to Principalship by Grade Level

	1980 Total	7-8-9	7-8	6-7-8	5-6-7-8	Other
Elementary teacher	2	1	2	1	0	4
Middle level teacher	12	7	15	11	33	16
High school teacher	8	9	6	7	5	11
Assistant principal of an elementary school	2	1	2	7	0	2
Assistant principal of a middle level school	29	37	25	26	0	27
Assistant principal of a high school	18	20	20	10	19	14
Principal of an elementary school	12	9	13	17	14	9
Principal of a high school	7	6	6	11	14	4
Guidance counselor	2	3	2	5	0	2
Central office administrator	3	2	4	3	5	4
Other	5	5	5	2	10	7

elementary or middle level school assistant principals. Perhaps this simply reflects the scarcity of such positions.

Years in the Last Position

The typical middle level principal has had from 4 to 14 years' experience in the previous position before coming to a middle level principalship. Table 32 indicates that 38 percent had 3 or less years' experience in their last position. No comparable data from previous studies are available.

Thirty-nine percent of the males and 53 percent of the females reported six or more years' experience prior to the middle level principalship (see Table 33). These data are consistent with the earlier data on age, experience, and sex.

TABLE 32
Years in Last Position Prior to Middle Level Principalship

Years	Middle Level 1980
1	10
2-3	28
4-5	22
6-7	20
8-9	5
10+	15

TABLE 33
Years in Last Position by Sex

Years	1980 Total	Male	Female
1	10	10	12
2-3	28	29	26
4-5	22	23	9
6-7	20	19	26
8-9	5	5	2
10+	15	14	25

Years Teaching Experience Prior to Present Position

Table 34 points out that 18 percent of elementary principals and 8 percent of middle level principals had only 3 or less years of teaching experience before assuming their present positions. More than half of all middle level principals fall in the range of 7 to 14 years of previous teaching experience.

Females have had more teaching experience than males. Table 35 establishes that 63 percent of the women principals have taught 10 or more years. Only 43 percent of the men show that much experience. Again, these figures parallel previously reported data.

TABLE 34
Years Teaching Prior to Present Position

Years	Middle Level 1980	Junior High 1966	Elementary Years	1979
<3	8	10	0	18
4-6	24	23	1	4
7-9	25	21	2-9	53
10-14	28	21	10-19	22
15+	15	25	20+	3

TABLE 35
Years of Teaching Experience by Sex

Years	1980 Total	Male	Female
<3	8	7	4
4-9	49	50	33
10+	43	43	63

Undergraduate College or University

In 1980 as in 1966, most principals attended a public university or college for their undergraduate work. By 1980, there was a slight increase in attendance at public institutions and a corresponding decline at private colleges or universities. Table 36 indicates that 69 percent of the middle level principals graduated from public colleges or universities. In the 1966 study, 64 percent of the junior high principals had attended public institutions.

TABLE 36
Undergraduate College

Type of College or University	1980	1966
Public	69	64
Private—Religiously affiliated	23	26
Private—Not religiously affiliated	7	10
Other	1	0

Major Field of Undergraduate Study

Table 37 shows that social science was the undergraduate major of the largest percentage of principals. The table also shows that the number of humanities majors had dropped at the middle level from 24 percent in 1966 to 7 percent in 1980. Only 15 percent of the respondents were physical education majors. Eleven percent majored in elementary education.

TABLE 37
Major Field of Undergraduate Study

	Middle Level 1980	Junior High 1966	Senior High 1978
Secondary education (other than physical education)	11 }	19	12
Elementary education	11 }		
Physical education	15	12	17
Humanities (literature, languages, etc.)	7	24	12
Physical and biological sciences	11	16	20
Social sciences (sociology, history, etc.)	22	15	26
Mathematics	7	—	—
Fine Arts	3	3	3
Business	5	5	7
Vocational-Technical (home ec., industrial arts, etc.)	5	—	—
Other	4	6	2
Engineering (1965 study only)	—	1	—

FIGURE B (Based on Table 38)
Undergraduate Major by Grade Level

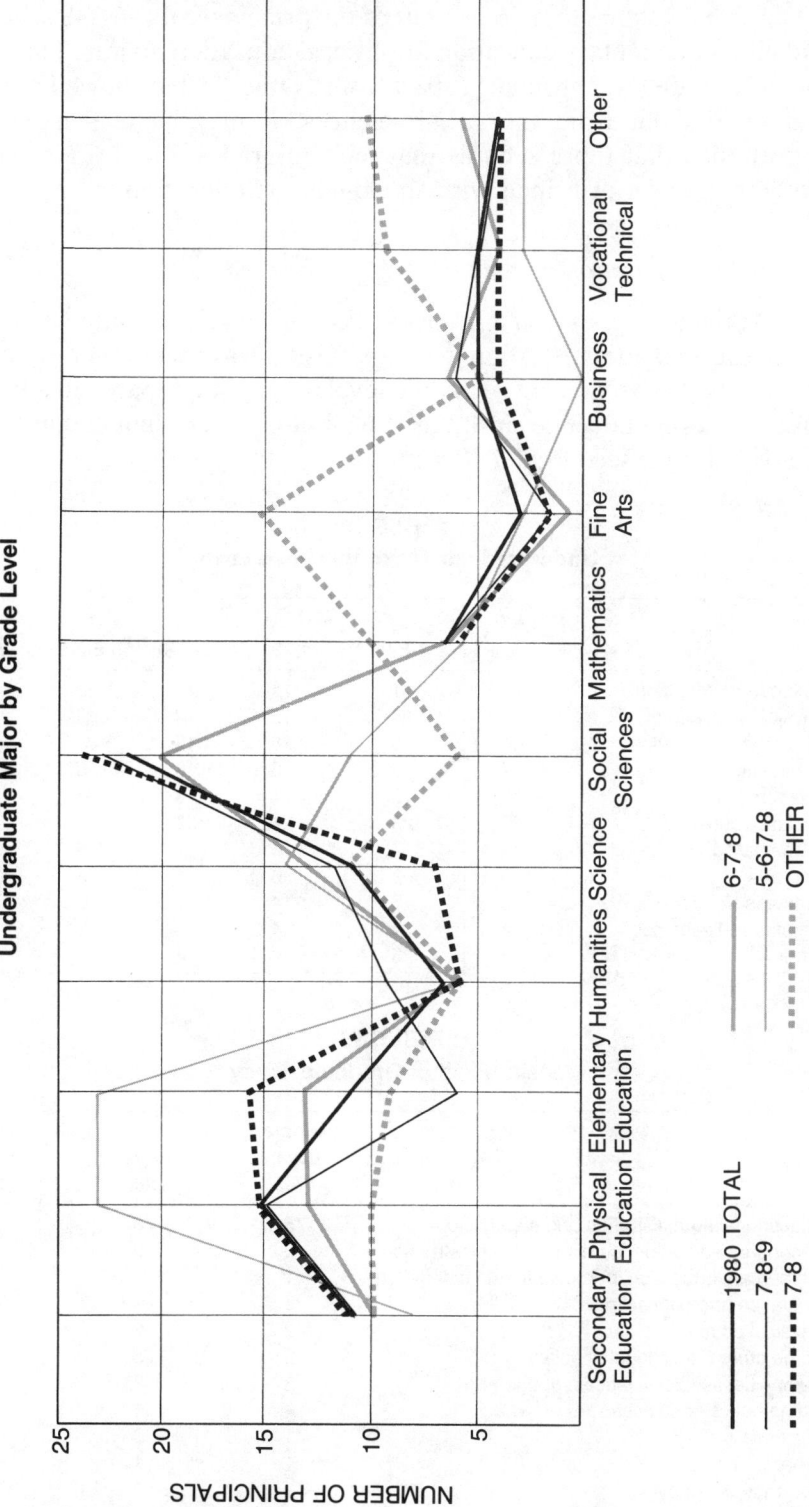

Table 38 shows that 46 percent of the principals of 5-6-7-8 schools had either elementary education or physical education majors. This was the only grade level grouping (apart from "Other") that showed prevalent majors not from the social sciences. It may be reasonable to hypothesize that those schools that include grades 5 and 6 are more likely to look for principals with an elementary education background.

Graduate Preparation

At the middle as well as at the senior high levels, a graduate major in educational administration and supervision was predominant. Table 39 reports that 75 percent of middle level principals prepared in administration, a slight decline since the 1966 study. Curriculum and instruction is a distant second at 7 percent.

TABLE 38
Undergraduate Major by Grade Level

	1980 Total	7-8-9	7-8	6-7-8	5-6-7-8	Other
Secondary education	11	11	11	10	8	10
Physical education	15	15	15	13	23	10
Elementary education	11	6	16	13	23	9
Humanities	7	9	6	6	6	6
Science	11	12	7	13	14	11
Social sciences	22	23	24	20	11	6
Mathematics	7	7	6	7	6	10
Fine arts	3	2	3	1	3	15
Business	5	6	4	7	0	5
Vocational-Technical	4	4	4	6	3	10
Other	5	5	4	4	3	9

TABLE 39
Major Field of Graduate Study

	Middle Level 1980	Junior High 1966	Senior High 1978
Educational administration and supervision	75	78	71
Secondary education, curriculum, and instruction	6	9	9
Elementary education, curriculum, and instruction	1	—	—
Guidance and counseling	5	—	—
Physical education	2	2	2
Some other educational specialty	2	5	7
Humanities, social sciences, or fine arts	3	3	4
Mathematics or sciences	4	1	3
Business	<1	0	0
Other	1	1	3
No graduate study	<1	1	0

TABLE 40
Highest Degree Earned

	Middle Level 1980	Junior High 1966	Senior High 1978	Elementary 1979
Bachelor's degree	1	6	1	3.6
Master's degree in education	23	33	12	
Master's degree not in education	1	2	2	74
Master's degree plus additional graduate work	49	47	56	
Educational specialist, six-year program, or equivalent	10	—	9	17.5
Master's degree plus all course work for a doctorate	7	7	9	—
Doctor of Education	5	3	9	4.9
Doctor of Philosophy	3	1		
Some other degree	1	1	2	

TABLE 41
Highest Earned Degree by Sex

	1980 Total	Male	Female
Bachelor's	1	1	4
Master's	80	81	65
Specialist	10	10	11
Doctorate	8	7	18
Other	1	1	2

Highest Degree Earned

Table 40 indicates an increase since 1966 in the formal preparation of principals at the middle level. Seventy-five percent of the 1980 respondents indicated work beyond the master's degree. In 1966 it was 59 percent. This may reflect simply the increased licensing requirements for principals throughout the country, but the trend is a promising one. Virtually all principals now report a master's degree or higher.

Table 41 shows that 18 percent of the female respondents have attained the doctorate against only 7 percent for males. It is interesting to note that female middle level principals are older, more experienced, and academically better prepared than their male counterparts.

Tables 42 and 43 deal with degree level by school configuration and enrollment.

A higher percentage of principals of 7-8-9 schools hold the doctorate—11 percent—than those of schools with other grade patterns (Table 42).

Principals in schools of 1,000 students or more have doctorates more commonly than the total sample. It appears that larger schools in

TABLE 42
Highest Earned Degree by Grade Level

	1980 Total	7-8-9	7-8	6-7-8	5-6-7-8	Other
Bachelor's	1	1	2	1	0	2
Master's	24	20	28	30	20	26
Master's plus	66	67	64	65	69	63
Doctorate	8	11	6	2	3	6
Other	1	1	0	2	8	3

TABLE 43
Highest Earned Degree by Enrollment

	1980 Total	<400	400-599	600-799	800-999	1,000-1,399	1,400+
Bachelor's	1	4	2	1	1	0	0
Master's in education	23	24	26	18	21	18	87
Master's not in education	1	1	1	3	1	0	0
Master's plus	49	52	49	50	50	45	7
Specialist	10	5	9	13	11	11	0
All but degree	7	8	6	7	8	8	0
Ed.D.	5	2	4	5	4	12	6
Ph.D.	3	<1	3	2	3	5	0
Other	1	2	0	1	1	1	0

TABLE 44
Administrative Certification

Type of License	Middle Level 1980
Secondary	66
Middle	8
Elementary	7
No building level certification	6
Other	13

larger districts more frequently seek out principals with that degree than smaller schools and/or smaller districts.

Administrative Certification

Most principals of schools in the middle have a *secondary* school principal license (Table 44). Few states, at this time, mandate a specific certificate for administrators of middle level schools; but some trend toward this does seem apparent. The typical state requirement today is still a secondary or an elementary license.

Table 45 indicates that considerably more female principals have elementary school administrative certification than do males. This is consistent with the data showing the highest percentage of female principals in schools that do not include the ninth grade, but do include grades 5 and/or 6.

Table 46 points out that 8 percent of the respondents have middle level certification. There is a marked decline in the percentage of principals holding secondary school principal's certification in those schools with lower grade levels.

Twenty-two percent of the 5-6-7-8 grade school principals are elementary-school licensed. Only 2 percent of the principals of 7-8-9 schools have that certificate.

Table 47 reveals a definite relationship between the size of student enrollment and secondary school administrative certification on the part of the principal. Only 55 percent of the principals of schools with enrollments of 400 or fewer have such a license (15 percent have elementary school administrative certification). In schools of 1,000 or more the figure jumps to 70 percent. Middle level certification also increases with school size.

TABLE 45
Administrative Certification by Sex

Type of License	1980 Total	Male	Female
Secondary	66	67	42
Middle	8	8	8
Elementary	7	7	19
No building level certification	6	6	11
Other	13	12	20

TABLE 46
Administrative Certification by Grade Level

	1980 Total	7-8-9	7-8	6-7-8	5-6-7-8	Other
Secondary	66	77	61	51	30	65
Middle	8	7	8	10	9	11
Elementary	7	2	9	14	22	9
No building level certification	6	4	8	8	14	6
Other	13	10	14	17	25	9

TABLE 47
Administrative Certification by Enrollment

	1980 Total	<400	400-599	600-799	800-999	1,000-1,399	1,400+
Secondary	66	55	62	70	68	72	70
Middle	8	7	9	6	10	7	17
Elementary	7	15	9	6	3	5	0
No building level certification	6	9	6	6	7	5	12
Other	13	14	14	12	12	11	1

FIGURE C (Based on Table 47)
Administrative Certification by Enrollment

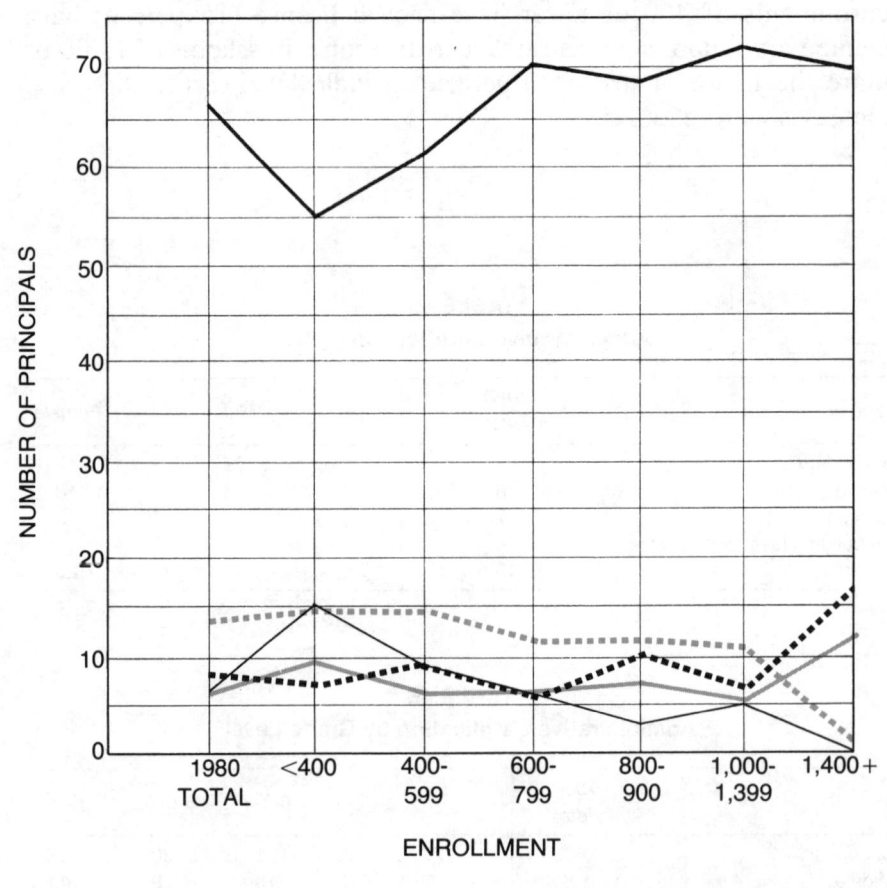

—— SECONDARY
········ MIDDLE
—— ELEMENTARY
—— NO BUILDING LEVEL CERTIFICATION
········ OTHER

Salary

Tables 48 and 49 outline salary data. Four-fifths of middle level principals report a salary between $20,000 and $34,000. Only 10 percent earn more than $35,000 per year. Seventeen percent of the female principals earn less than $20,000 annually compared to 6 percent for males. The fact that more women are new to the position may be relevant in evaluating this differential.

FIGURE D (Based on Table 48)   Principals' Annual Salary

- More than $40,000: 2%
- Less than $15,000: 1%
- $15,000-19,999: 5%
- $35,000-39,999: 8%
- $20,000-24,999: 26%
- $30,000-34,999: 26%
- $25,000-29,999: 32%

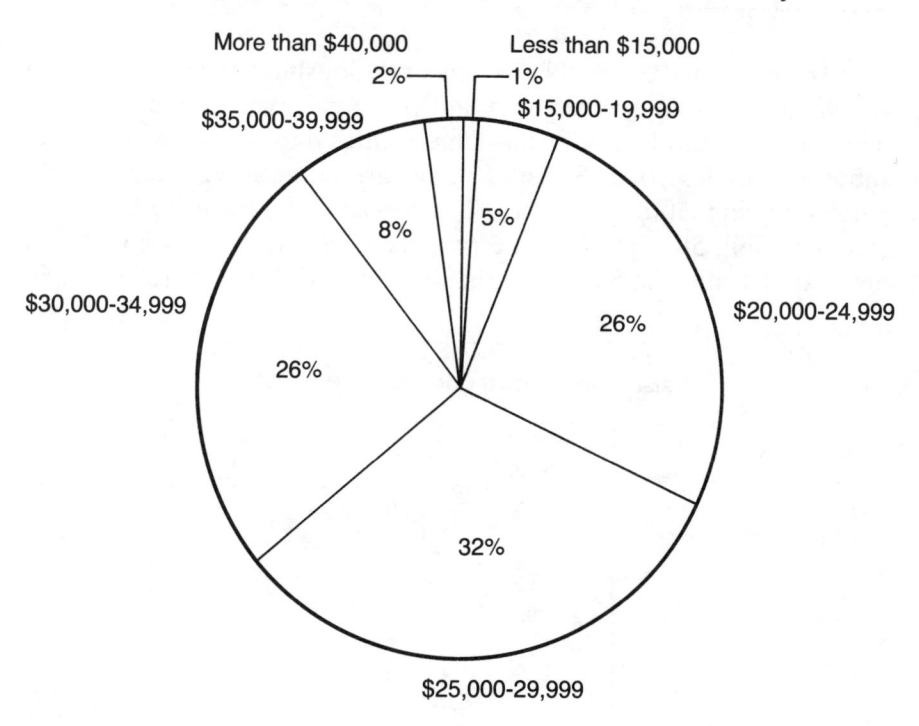

TABLE 48
Current Annual Salary

<$10,000	<1
$10,000–$14,999	1
$15,000–$19,999	5
$20,000–$24,999	26
$25,000–$29,999	32
$30,000–$34,999	26
$35,000–$39,999	8
$40,000–$44,999	2
$45,000+	<1

TABLE 49
Salary by Sex

	Total	Male	Female
<$10,000	<1	<1	6
$10,000-$14,999	1	<1	3
$15,000-$19,999	5	5	8
$20,000-$24,999	26	26	24
$25,000-$29,999	32	32	25
$30,000-$34,999	26	26	26
$35,000-$39,999	8	8	6
$40,000-$44,999	2	2	1
$45,000+	1	1	1

Tables 50 and 51 verify a positive relationship between salary and the variables of community size and per-pupil expenditure. Only 12 percent of the principals in the largest cities and 9 percent from the suburbs earn less than $25,000 per year. In rural communities, 61 percent are in that range. In those districts annually spending $1,200 or less per pupil, 50 percent of the principals earn less than $25,000. In high expenditure districts, those that allocate $1,800 or more per pupil,

TABLE 50
Salary Based upon Community Population

	1980 Total	City of 150,000+	Suburban	25,000-149,999	5,000-24,999	Rural
<$15,000	1	3	0	0	1	1
$15,000-19,999	5	0	1	3	5	16
$20,000-24,999	26	9	8	20	41	44
$25,000-29,999	32	32	30	34	36	28
$30,000-34,999	26	35	41	33	14	9
$35,000-39,999	9	17	16	9	2	1
$40,000+	2	4	4	1	1	1

TABLE 51
Salary by Per-Pupil Expenditure

	1980 Total	<$1,200	$1,200-1,799	$1,800+
<$10,000	<1	1	1	0
$10,000-14,999	1	2	1	0
$15,000-19,999	5	9	3	2
$20,000-24,999	26	38	20	9
$25,000-29,999	32	27	38	17
$30,000-34,999	26	19	29	35
$35,000-39,999	8	2	6	27
$40,000-44,999	2	1	1	9
$45,000+	<1	1	1	1

only 11 percent of the principals earn that little. Predictably, the largest and richest districts pay the largest salaries.

Basis of Salary Determination

Sixty-five percent of the respondents indicated that their salary was determined on a basis separate from that of the teachers' salary schedule. Table 52 shows that 40 percent of the principals in rural areas have their salaries tied to those of teachers. This is the traditional practice. The likelihood of a separate administrators' salary contract is greater in the suburbs and in the large cities than in other categories. The growing phenomenon of states allowing principals to bargain collectively for themselves contributes to increasing salary schedule autonomy.

Length of Salary Contract

The length of principals' contracts has been extended since the 1966 study. Presently only 10 percent have contracts less than 10½ months. In 1966 the figure was 26 percent. Table 53 indicates that the modal response, 47 percent, is a 12 month contract. The Middle Atlantic states have the highest incidence of 12 month contracts (75 percent); the Rocky Mountain region, the highest percentage of 10½ month contracts (29 percent).

Tenure as a Principal

The percentage of tenured principals is down 10 points since 1966, from 45 to 35 percent (Table 54). This is a bit surprising in view of the fact that 1980 principals are slightly older than their 1966 counterparts.

TABLE 52
Basis for Salary Determination by Population

	1980 Total	City of 150,000+	Suburban	25,000-149,999	5,000-24,999	Rural
Percentage of teacher	15	16	11	16	16	16
Teacher plus	15	11	9	14	17	24
Separate administrator negotiation	36	48	46	33	35	27
Individual negotiation	6	0	3	6	5	13
Nonnegotiated administrator schedule	23	22	25	27	23	12
DNA	1	3	1	1	1	0
Other	4	0	5	3	3	8

TABLE 53
Length of Salary Contract

Months	Middle Level 1980	Junior High 1966	Elementary 1979
12	47	36	30
11½	<1	} 37	17
11	28		
10½	15		44
10	10		
9½	<1	} 26	7
9	0		

Table 55 indicates that 36 percent of the male middle level principals have tenure but only 21 percent of the females, perhaps because females have fewer years of experience as principals (see Table 24).

The highest percentage of tenured principals is found in grade 7-8-9 and 6-7-8 schools (Table 56). Principals of 7-8-9 schools are more experienced, however, than principals of schools with other grade configurations. Table 57 points out that principal tenure has greater prevalence in the Middle Atlantic states, at 72 percent, than in other areas of the country.

TABLE 54
Tenure as a Principal

	Middle Level 1980	Junior High 1966
Yes	35	45
No	65	55

TABLE 55
Tenure by Sex

	1980 Total	Male	Female
Yes	35	36	21
No	65	64	79

TABLE 56
Tenure by Grade Level

	1980 Total	7-8-9	7-8	6-7-8	5-6-7-8	Other
Yes	35	40	28	36	19	44
No	65	60	72	64	81	56

TABLE 57
Tenure by Region

	1980 Total	New England	Middle Atlantic	South	Mid-west	South-west	Rocky Mountain	Far West
Yes	35	50	72	47	20	27	23	22
No	65	50	28	53	80	73	77	78

TABLE 58
Participation in Professional Activities

Degrees of Participation	Studies at Higher Ed. Institutions 1980	Studies at Higher Ed. Institutions 1966	Participated in Activities of Professional Associations 1980	Participated in Activities of Professional Associations 1966
Very extensively	9		15	
Extensively	17	35	39	53
Slightly	33		40	
Not at all	41	65	6	47

TABLE 59
Participation in Higher Education Studies by Sex

	1980 Total	Male	Female
Extensively	26	26	42
Little or none	74	74	58

Participation in Professional Activities

Respondents were asked to what extent they participated in professional activities during the past two years. Since 1966, the percentage has increased—35 to 59 percent in "Study at Colleges or Universities," and 53 to 94 percent in "Activities of Professional Associations," (Table 58). Perhaps more states and districts are mandating continual professional growth. More female principals than males reported extensive participation in higher education programs. This finding is consistent with a greater incidence of earned doctorates among female administrators.

Table 60 establishes a positive relationship between degree earned and participation in professional association activities. Only 22 percent of principals with a bachelor's degree as their most advanced work reported extensive involvement as opposed to 64 percent of those with a doctorate.

TABLE 60
Participation in Activities of Professional Associations by Highest Degree

	1980 Total	Bachelor's	Master's	Specialist	Doctor's	Other
Extensively	54	22	52	63	64	56
Little or none	46	78	48	37	36	44

TABLE 61
Number of Civic and Political Organization Memberships

Number	Middle Level 1980	Junior High 1966
None	34	25
One	29	31
Two	23	26
Three	8	11
Four or more	6	7

Civic and Political Organization Memberships

Principals were asked to indicate the number of civic and political organizations (Chamber of Commerce, Rotary, etc.) in which they presently hold membership. Fewer indicated such affiliation in 1980 than in 1966. Eighty-one percent of the women reported active membership to 64 percent for the men. Principals in large cities were less active than those in other population categories. Only 54 percent of the large city principals belonged to one or more civic and political organizations. Perhaps the greater time demands of the job have contributed to this decline in community-related activity.

Principal's Career Aspirations

Principals are more upwardly mobile than in the 1966 study (Table 62). Central office aspirations have increased in popularity since that time. A position in the central office is the career goal of 26 percent of the respondents. Thirty-seven percent said they were happy to remain in their present positions as middle level principals, down from 51 percent in the 1966 study. Thirty-three percent of the female principals were undecided about their career futures; only 17 percent of the males were uncertain. More males than females aspired to central office positions.

TABLE 62
Principal's Career Aspirations

	Middle Level 1980	Junior High 1966	Senior High 1978
Yes, to a middle level principalship in a larger district	1	—	4*
Yes, to a middle level principalship in a smaller district	<1	—	0*
Yes, to a high school principalship	7	9	—
Yes, to an elementary school principalship	2	—	—
Yes, to a superintendency or central office position	26	16	33
Yes, to a junior college, college, or university position	2	8	5
Yes, to some other position in education	2	—	5
I am undecided	18	—	20
No, I hope to remain in my present position	37	51	28
No, I hope to take a position outside of education	5	—	—
Other (1966 study only)	—	17	—
Yes, to teaching or counseling (1978 study only)	—	—	5

*Reference point is the *senior* high principalship.

TABLE 63
Principal's Career Aspirations by Sex

Position	Total	Male	Female
Yes, to a middle level principalship in a larger district	1	1	2
Yes, to a middle level principalship in a smaller district	<1	<1	0
Yes, to a high school principalship	7	7	12
Yes, to an elementary school principalship	2	2	0
Yes, to a superintendency or central office position	26	27	12
Yes, to a college position	2	2	9
Yes, to some other position in education	2	2	2
I am undecided	18	17	33
No, I hope to remain in my present position	37	37	28
No, I hope to take a position outside of education	5	5	2

The highest percentage of those who prefer to remain in the middle level principalship supervise schools with grades 6-7-8, as reported in Table 64. Later in this study, we will document that the 6-7-8 grade configuration is the most popular organizational pattern among the survey respondents, regardless of the grade levels of their present assignments.

TABLE 64
Principal's Career Aspirations by Grade Level

	1980 Total	7-8-9	7-8	6-7-8	5-6-7-8	Other
Yes, larger district	1	2	1	2	0	2
Yes, smaller district	<1	<1	0	0	0	0
High school principal	7	11	4	4	0	11
Elementary principal	2	1	2	2	5	2
Central office	26	28	29	16	43	16
College position	2	<1	3	8	5	0
Other education position	2	1	2	2	5	0
Undecided	18	16	20	16	14	18
No, remain here	37	33	35	48	24	44
No, outside education	5	7	4	2	4	7

Career Choice

Respondents were asked, "If you could choose again, would you select educational administration as a career?" The data indicate that 68 percent would do so (see Table 65). This percentage is slightly higher than in the 1966 study, at 64 percent. Perhaps the principalship at the middle level is less stressful than it was in the earlier decade. Certainly 80 percent of the female principals would make the same choice again, and 68 percent of the males. Table 66, in fact, documents that only a small percentage would clearly opt for something else.

TABLE 65
Commitment to Same Career Choice

	Middle Level 1980	Junior High 1966	Senior High 1978	Elementary 1979
Definitely yes	41	64	37	49
Probably yes	27		32	34
Uncertain	15	24	15	—
Probably no	14	12	12	4
Definitely no	3		3	3

TABLE 66
Commitment to Same Career Choice by Sex

	1980 Total	Male	Female
Definitely yes	41	40	58
Probably yes	27	28	22
Uncertain	15	15	4
Probably no	14	14	9
Definitely no	3	3	7

Summary

PERSONAL FACTORS

The 1980 study profiles a typical middle level principal as a white male between the ages of 45 and 54. The percentage of females in the middle level principalship has increased from 4 percent in the 1966 study to 6 percent currently. On the other hand, the percentage of females in the senior high and elementary studies decreased over the time span of those studies.

Data indicate that 8 percent of middle level principals are nonwhite. At the senior high level the figure is 4 percent; at the elementary level, 9.3 percent. The 1980 study shows that 17 percent of the female middle level principals are nonwhite.

A higher percentage of minority principals are found in large schools, in large cities, and in the South and Far West.

PROFESSIONAL FACTORS

The typical middle level principal was appointed to his/her first principalship between the ages of 30 and 39. Females were appointed at a slightly older age than males.

Half the respondents were in their first principalship and moved to the position from an assistant principalship after 4-14 years of teaching experience.

Most middle level principals received their undergraduate degree from a public university or college. Social sciences was the most frequently reported undergraduate major.

At the graduate level, a major in educational administration and supervision was the most prevalent.

In 1980, 74 percent of the respondents indicated formal graduate work beyond the master's degree. In 1966, the figure was 59 percent. More females than males have earned the doctorate. Virtually all principals hold a master's degree or higher.

Most principals of middle level schools have a secondary school principal's license. They earn salaries between $20,000 and $34,999, on schedules not tied to the teacher scales, and for 10½ months or longer.

The percentage who are tenured as principals has declined since the 1966 study—from 45 percent in 1965 to 35 percent in 1980.

More principals in 1980 than in 1966 participated in professional activities, including advanced graduate study and increased participation in activities of their professional organizations. Participation in civic and political organizations has decreased—from 75 to 66 percent.

Most respondents indicated that they would make the same career choice again and many wanted to remain middle level principals. If they aspired to a change, a position in the central office was the most attractive.

II. Tasks and Problems of the Middle Level Principal

Schools in the middle have attracted continual attention since they were first created in the early 1900s. A major focus has been the role of the principal. What does the principal do? How long does the principal work? What are the principal's priorities? What are the roadblocks to the successful completion of the principal's tasks?

This chapter provides information that will help answer these questions.

ACTIVITIES AND TASKS

Typical Work Week

The typical middle level principal puts in a work week of over 50 hours, as shown in Table 67. The senior high school principal's week is even longer with a median of 56.5 hours (reported in the 1978 NASSP study). The 1979 NAESP study reports a 45-hour work week for the typical elementary school principal. The time spent on the job has not changed significantly for the middle level principal since 1966.

TABLE 67
Average Work Week of Principals

Hours per week	Middle Level 1980	Junior High 1966	Senior High 1978
<40	1	4	0
40-49	27	27	17
50-59	55	54	61
60-69	15	12	22
70+	2	3	

TABLE 68
Average Work Week by Sex

	1980 Total	Male	Female
<40	1	1	0
40-49	27	28	15
50-59	55	55	61
60-69	15	15	20
70+	2	1	4

Table 68 points out that 85 percent of female principals work more than 50 hours a week; 71 percent of the males do so.

Allocation of Time for a Typical Work Week

Principals were asked to describe how they *do* spend time and how they felt they *should* spend their time. The results of their rank ordering of nine areas of responsibility are presented in Table 69. These rankings are based on the median scores in each area. A rank of 1 indicates the greatest amount of time spent; 9 indicates the least amount of time.

Respondents at both the middle and senior high levels declared program development their number one priority. Yet in both the 1980 and 1978 studies they reported that school management was the most time-demanding facet of their job. Principals would like planning activities to receive more attention. They agree on the "should" and "do" of personnel administration. It seems safe to assume from those data that "managerial" demands detract from the "leadership" functions of the principal. This tendency will be a matter of some concern to those who would prefer principals to be positive change agents.

Teaching Responsibility of Principals

Table 70 reveals a higher percentage of 1980 middle level principals (at 96 percent) who report no regular teaching responsibilities than among the 1966 study respondents (89 percent). This trend also closely parallels the size of the schools. Only in the smallest schools do the principals have teaching responsibilities of any significance. The size of the typical middle level school appears to be growing in all parts of the country, and, with size, administrative duties become more demanding. Consequently, instruction is increasingly left to the teaching staff.

TABLE 69
Rank Order of Time Allocation for a Typical Work Week

Area of Responsibility	Middle Level 1980-Do Spend Time	Middle Level 1980-Should Spend Time	Senior High 1978-Do Spend Time	Senior High 1978-Should Spend Time
Program development	4	1	5	1
Personnel	2	2	2	2
School management	1	3	1	3
Student activities	5	4	3	4
Student behavior	3	8	4	7
Community	7	6	8	8
District office	6	9	6	9
Professional development	9	7	9	6
Planning	8	5	7	5

FIGURE E (Based on Table 69) Typical Work Week of Middle-Level Principals

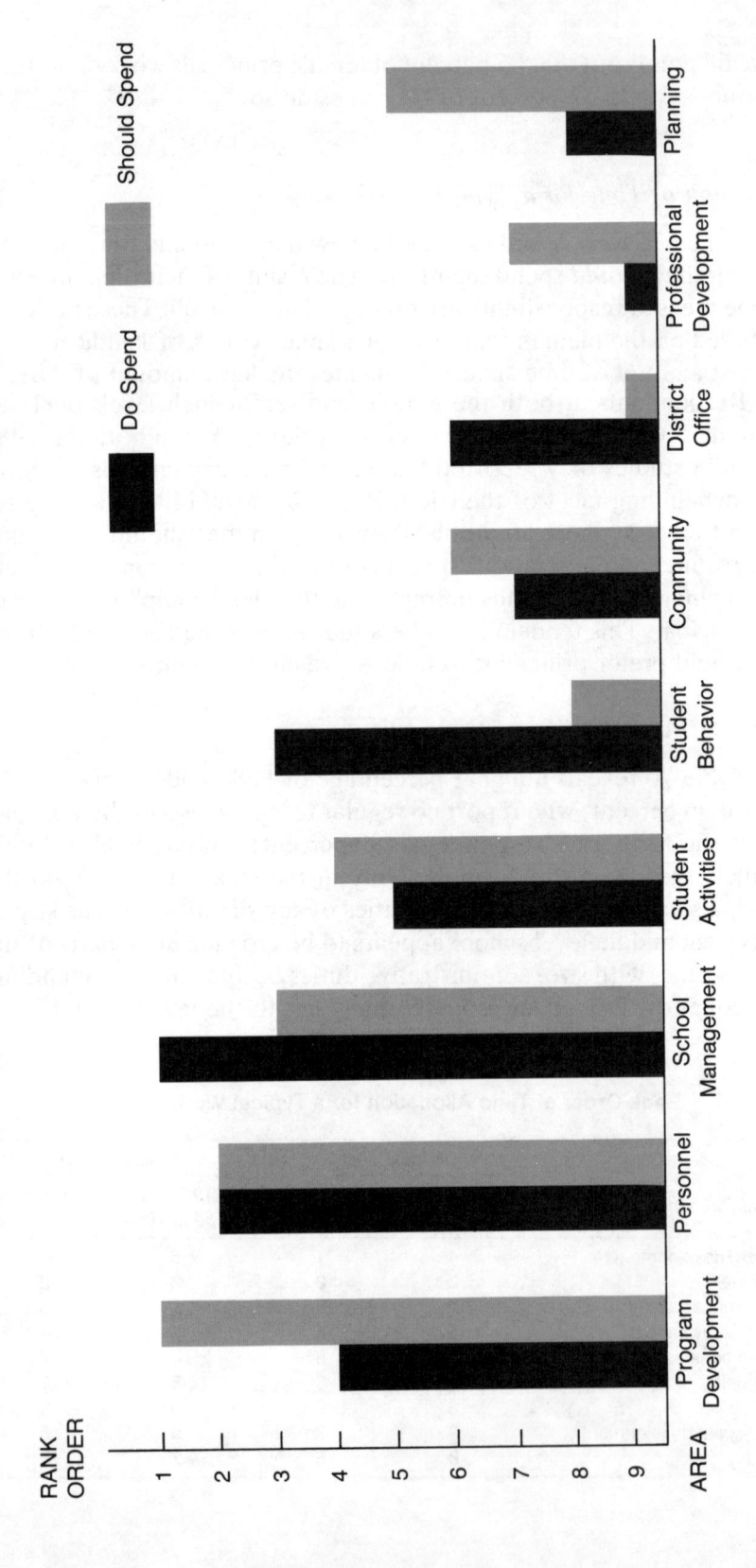

TABLE 70
Teaching Responsibilities

Number of Courses	Middle Level 1980	Junior High 1966	Senior High 1978
None	96	89	85
One	2	5 ⎫	13
Two+	2	6 ⎭	

JOB CHARACTERISTICS

Five questions required the respondents to consider certain aspects of the middle level principalship: prestige of the position, the opportunity for independent thought and actions, self-fulfillment of the position, job security, and the principalship as an opportunity to help others. Reaction to these factors in the "ideal" column suggests that they should be in much greater evidence than they actually are at present.

Table 71 makes clear that the 1980 respondents felt more actual prestige than did their counterparts in the 1966 study. Ninety-five percent of the middle level principals reported moderate to much prestige. In the 1966 study the figure was 84 percent. Obviously, there is a slight improvement in the respondent's sense of self-fulfillment since 1966. In the areas of job security and the opportunity to help others, middle level principals perceived themselves more favorably than their senior high counterparts. Female principals felt even better about the prestige factor than males; 70 percent said they enjoyed "much" prestige as compared to 54 percent for men.

Table 73 indicates that there is an interesting relationship between feelings of self-fulfillment and salary. Thirty-one percent of the principals earning $40,000 or more reported much self-fulfillment. This was the highest response in any of the salary categories except for the "Less than $15,000" column. Some say that salary has little to do with job satisfaction, but these data suggest that salary may make a difference. Those in the lowest salary range may be principals of private or parochial schools where considerations other than salary may be preeminent.

Table 74 shows that levels of satisfaction are reasonably high for principals in all grade level combinations. Those in 5-6-7-8 schools and the "other" category expressed the highest satisfaction with their work (71 percent). Interestingly, the lowest figure in the "much self-fulfillment" category (21 percent) is found in 7-8-9 schools, the traditional junior high organizational structure.

Those who would make the same career choice felt more self-fulfillment—78 percent—than did those who were unsure—56 per-

TABLE 71
Principals' Rating of Job Characteristics

Rating	Middle Level Actual 1980	Middle Level Ideal 1980	Junior High Actual 1966	Senior High Actual 1978	Senior High Ideal 1978
Prestige					
1 (Little)	1	0	3	1	0
2	4	1	13	4	0
3 (Moderate)	40	18	50	30	18
4	42	58	30	35	41
5 (Much)	13	23	4	30	40
Independent Thought and Action					
1 (Little)	3	0	—	2	0
2	6	0	—	10	0
3 (Moderate)	31	5	—	34	7
4	41	56	—	33	43
5 (Much)	19	39	—	21	50
Self-Fulfillment					
1 (Little)	1	0	2	2	0
2	6	0	8	7	0
3 (Moderate)	28	3	24	30	3
4	40	36	49	33	31
5 (Much)	25	61	18	27	66
Job Security					
1 (Little)	5	0	—	10	1
2	5	1	—	7	1
3 (Moderate)	21	14	—	25	20
4	35	37	—	31	43
5 (Much)	34	48	—	31	43
Opportunity To Help Others					
1 (Little)	0	0	—	1	0
2	1	0	—	2	0
3 (Moderate)	15	2	—	21	4
4	32	24	—	30	25
5 (Much)	52	74	—	46	71

TABLE 72
Actual Prestige of Position by Sex

	1980 Total	Male	Female
Little	5	5	2
Moderate	40	41	28
Much	55	54	70

TABLE 73
Self-Fulfillment Based upon Salary

Scale	1980 Totals	<15,000	$15,000-$19,999	$20,000-$24,999	$25,000-$29,999	$30,000-$34,999	$35,000-$39,999	$40,000+
1 Little	1	0	0	2	1	1	1	0
2	6	14	10	5	6	6	9	7
3 Moderate	28	22	37	29	28	24	26	28
4	40	22	37	40	40	43	36	34
5 Much	25	42	16	24	25	26	28	31

TABLE 74
Self-Fulfillment Based upon Grade Level

Scale	1980 Totals	7-8-9	7-8	6-7-8	5-6-7-8	Other
1 (Little)	1	1	1	0	2	2
2	6	6	6	8	4	6
3 (Moderate)	28	31	28	20	24	21
4	40	40	40	29	41	42
5 (Much)	25	21	25	33	30	29

TABLE 75
Self-Fulfillment Based upon Same Career Choice

Self-Fulfillment	1980 Total	Yes	Unknown	No
Little	7	4	9	17
Moderate	28	18	35	38
Much	65	78	56	45

cent—or those who had decided not to make the same career choice—45 percent (Table 75).

AUTHORITY IN DECISION MAKING

Autonomy in Staffing Practices

Several questions in the study deal with principal's authority or extent of participation in the decision-making processes of the school. One question asks, "How much authority do you have to make personnel decisions such as employing one full-time teacher or an alternative; e.g., two or three teacher aides?" The responses are found in Table 76. Middle level principals have less unrestricted authority to act than do senior high principals or elementary school principals. Generally speaking, however, principals do have considerable control over staffing in their own buildings. No more than a third at any level expressed a sense of little or no control.

TABLE 76
Authority in Staffing Practices

Authority	Middle Level 1980	Senior High 1978	Elementary 1979
Unrestricted	5	16	43
With some restrictions	62	51	38
Little	20	20 }	19
None	13	12 }	

Table 77 reveals a strong correlation between feelings of self-fulfillment and authority in staffing practices. Of those who experience much self-fulfillment in the principalship, 73 percent report little or no restrictions in their staffing authority. Of those with little sense of fulfillment, only 40 percent indicate that they are relatively unrestricted. Apparently authority to act and self-fulfillment are intimately related.

Table 78 reports responses to the question, "How much authority do you have to fill teacher vacancies?" Since the 1966 study, principals have been given greater authority to make this kind of decision. In 1966, 20 percent had this authority; in 1980, the figure had increased to 33 percent. Forty-eight percent of the principals in schools with grades 5-6-7-8 reported that they had authority to make such staffing deci-

TABLE 77
Authority in Staffing Practices by Self-Fulfillment

Authority	1980 Total	Self-Fulfillment Little	Moderate	Much
Unrestricted or some restrictions	67	40	57	73
Little or none	33	60	43	27

TABLE 78
Authority To Fill Teacher Vacancies

	Middle Level 1980	Junior High 1966	Senior High 1978
I make the selection and the central office endorses it.	33	20	51
I make the selection within limited options stipulated by the central office.	32 }	60	41
I recommend a person to fill the vacancy and the central office makes the decision.	26 }		
The central office selects the teacher to fill the vacancy.	9	19	8
Other (1966 study only)	—	1	—

sions. This is the highest response by a rather notable degree. Principals in rural areas have the most staffing authority (43 percent); those in the largest cities have the least (12 percent). It may be that larger districts more often have special personnel departments to handle this function.

Participation in Budget Matters

Principals were asked, "To what extent do you participate in determining the budget allocation for your school?" As shown in Table 79, only 23 percent of the principals have a high degree of participation in such decisions. Senior high principals appear to have a greater voice in such matters (37 percent). Those in cities of 150,000 or more have the least voice in budget allocation. Table 80 shows that 44 percent have no voice in budgeting and only 11 percent, the lowest response in the population categories, report a high level of participation. Large districts typically have a special central office to handle such matters—a position not commonly found in small districts.

Table 81 presents information in response to the question, "To what extent do you have authority to approve the allocation of discretionary funds within your school budget"; i.e., how much autonomy or latitude do you have in the allocation of monies that are already available to your building? At the middle level, 16 percent of the respondents have unrestricted authority in this area and 62 percent express

TABLE 79
Participation in Budget Allocation for School

Extent of Participation	Middle Level 1980	Senior High 1978
High	23	37
Moderate	40	30
Little	25	21
None	22	12

TABLE 80
Participation in Budget Allocation by Population

	1980 Total	City of 150,000+	Suburban	25,000-149,999	5,000-24,999	Rural
High	23	11	29	24	28	19
Moderate	30	17	30	30	31	33
Little	25	28	19	24	26	29
None	22	44	22	22	15	19

TABLE 81
Authority in Allocation of Discretionary Funds

Authority	Middle Level 1980	Senior High 1978
Unrestricted	16	19
Some restrictions	62	58
Little	16	16
None	6	6

TABLE 82
Authority in Allocation of Discretionary Funds by Self-Fulfillment

Authority	1980 Total	Self-Fulfillment Little	Moderate	Much
Unrestricted or some restrictions	78	57	66	84
Little or none	22	43	34	16

little restriction. Data are comparable for senior high principals. Authority in this area is correlated positively with respondents' feelings of self-fulfillment. Table 82 shows that 84 percent of those who experience much self-fulfillment in their positions are also relatively unrestricted in allocation of building funds; only 57 percent of those who indicate little self-fulfillment report a similar freedom.

ADMINISTRATIVE ROADBLOCKS

Table 83 summarizes rank-order data on factors considered to be "roadblocks" preventing principals from doing their jobs. The percentages reflect the number of principals who believed that the described condition was indeed an obstacle to the achievement of their job objectives. The most frequently reported roadblock was "time taken by administrative detail" (86 percent), also true in the 1978 Senior High study. "Apathetic or irresponsible parents" and "problem students" were the next most frequently mentioned factors. Size of school, whether large or small, was not seen as a significant problem.

These data corroborate the figures reported in Table 69 where management was ranked as the most demanding facet of the principal's work week.

TABLE 83
Administrative Roadblocks

Factors	Middle Level 1980	Junior High 1966	Senior High 1978
Time taken by administrative detail	86	32	90
Apathetic or irresponsible parents	78	—	79
Problem students	77	—	76
Inability to obtain funding	75	—	79
Lack of time for myself	75	—	86
Variations in the ability and dedication of staff	74	38	84
Resistance to change by staff	69	18	56
Defective communication among administrative levels	65	11	54
Time required to administrate and supervise extracurriculars	65	—	—
Lack of staff knowledge regarding middle level students	63	—	—
Collective bargaining agreement	58	—	41
Insufficient space and physical facilities	53	35	66
Longstanding traditions in the school/district	53	—	40
Pressure from community	52	—	—
Teacher tenure	52	12	50
Lack of districtwide flexibility	50	11	35
Inability to provide teacher planning or professional development time	49	—	59
Superintendent or central office staff who have not measured up to expectations	42	—	38
Teacher turnover	30	23	—
Lack of competent administrative assistance	30	—	—
Lack of competent office help	23	13	24
Too large a student body	19	—	20
Too small a student body	17	—	—

Summary

The typical middle level principal has an average work week of more than 50 hours. Females report a longer work week than males.

School management demands the most time of middle level principals even though they would prefer to spend the bulk of their time in program development.

Very few middle level principals have classroom teaching responsibilities.

Most principals feel their jobs are self-fulfilling, prestigious, and secure. Salary, autonomy in staffing practices, and authority in budget allocations relate positively to principals' sense of self-fulfillment.

In the areas of staffing authority and budget control, there is a negative relationship between these factors and the size of community or district in which the school is located. The larger the community/district, the less the authority.

"Administrative detail" is the major roadblock to principal job performance.

III Staff, Students, and Community

Involvement of staff, students, and community in the school program provides a stimulating challenge to principals. These groups have a legitimate expectation of involvement. In addition, federal and state programs frequently mandate their participation in the planning and operation of specific programs. Therefore, an understanding of the needs of the staff, the students, and the community is important to the effective principal.

This chapter focuses on each of these three groups. The background, preparation, and characteristics of teaching and support staff are analyzed. Schools are described in terms of student enrollment and average daily attendance; communities, in terms of population and location. Parental desire for involvement in the school program is documented. Finally, the roles of various individuals or groups in the decision-making process are discussed.

THE STAFF

The staff of a middle level school in 1980 is significantly different from the junior high staff of 1966. Table 84 presents a comparison of selected school staff in the 1966 NASSP Junior High School study and in this study, including a breakdown of 1980 data by grade level. The table gives the percentage of schools having one or more full-time employees in the selected categories.

TABLE 84
School Staff Availability

	1966 Total	1980 Total	1980 Grades 7-8-9	7-8	6-7-8	5-6-7-8
Assistant principal	42	77	91	67	71	38
Librarian/Media specialist	64	96	98	95	95	81
Office secretary/Clerks	76	99	100	100	99	100
Instructional aides	—	78	81	75	78	74
Nurses	15	61	72	62	71	59
Counselors	61	90	98	86	81	76
Special education teachers	—	97	97	95	98	97
Security/Supervisory aides	—	26	29	16	21	18

More than three of every four principals reported having an assistant principal contrasted with less than half so reporting 15 years ago. Principals typically felt that the number of assistant principals in the building and the quality of the administrative assistance in the school were adequate.

Significant staff increases have also occurred in the positions of librarian/media specialist, office secretaries, nurses, and counselors. Nearly every school has at least one special education teacher, the average number being slightly more than two and one-half per building. Most schools also have instructional aides, on the average slightly more than two per building. Schools with grades 7-8-9 typically have more support staff than those with other grade level patterns, probably because 7-8-9 buildings usually have larger enrollments. (The 1966 study did not report data on instructional aides, special education, or security personnel, so no comparisons are possible.)

When analyzed by the size of the community, schools in rural areas and communities of fewer than 25,000 population generally employed fewer staff members, and in particular, fewer assistant principals, counselors, and aides (Table 85). Undoubtedly this phenomenon is related to the smaller size of the schools in these settings.

Women represent the majority of teachers at the middle level. As shown in Table 85, the faculties of 62 percent of the schools surveyed had more female than male teachers. The predominance of females was true regardless of the grade level organization of the school, but was even more apparent in schools of grades 6-7-8 and 5-6-7-8.

Teacher Preparation and Service

In recent years the issue of preparation of teachers for the middle level has surfaced. When asked what level of educational preparation was most representative of teachers new to the building in the past five years, 77 percent of the principals indicated a bachelor's degree was

TABLE 85
School Staff by Community Population

	All schools 1980	City of 150,000+	Suburban	25,000-149,999	5,000-24,999	Rural
Assistant principal	77	95	92	94	70	33
Librarian/Media specialist	96	98	96	99	98	89
Office secretary/Clerks	99	100	100	99	99	98
Instructional aides	78	88	78	78	80	70
Nurses	61	59	72	63	59	51
Counselors	90	95	95	97	89	75
Special education teachers	97	92	99	97	97	95
Security/Supervisory aides	26	55	32	24	19	12

TABLE 86
Ratio of Female Teachers by Grade Level

	Total	7-8-9	7-8	6-7-8	5-6-7-8	Other
Schools with less than 50 percent female teachers	38	42	42	26	30	43
Schools with 50 percent or more female teachers	62	58	58	84	80	57

most common. Eight percent of the principals reported that the majority of their teachers had secondary certification; 9 percent indicated that elementary certification was most prevalent; and 11 percent that the majority of their teachers had middle level certification.

When asked whether faculty members, both new and existing, had specific preparation for working at the middle level (Table 87), 41 percent of the principals indicated their teachers had no specific middle level preparation. Table 88 shows the most common forms of preparation to be inservice programs, student teaching at the middle level, and university courses for the middle level.

A concern of middle level education has always been the number of teachers who leave the middle level for teaching positions in elementary or high schools. Principals were asked what percentage of their teachers were committed to teaching at the middle level as contrasted with those awaiting the opportunity to take a position at another level. Their responses show that a large majority of middle level teachers appear to like their work. Half of the principals indicated that at least 75 percent of their teachers wished to remain at the middle level.

TABLE 87
Teacher Preparation for Middle Level

No preparation	41
Some preparation	59

TABLE 88
Forms of Teacher Preparation

Inservice program	72
Student teaching in middle level schools	58
University courses for middle level	44
Personal or self-study	28
Preschool workshops	24

Teacher-Pupil Ratio

Teacher-pupil ratios were analyzed on the basis of grade organizational patterns, enrollment in the school, and per-pupil expenditure. Ratios differed very little on the basis of grade level. When analyzed by enrollment, however, obvious differences emerged (Table 89). Schools with fewer students had smaller ratios; larger schools, larger ratios. Nearly one-third of the largest schools had ratios in excess of 1:30.

Table 90 depicts teacher-pupil ratio by per-pupil expenditure. As might be anticipated, schools spending more money per pupil had smaller teacher-pupil ratios.

FIGURE F (Based on Table 89)
Teacher-Pupil Ratio by Enrollment

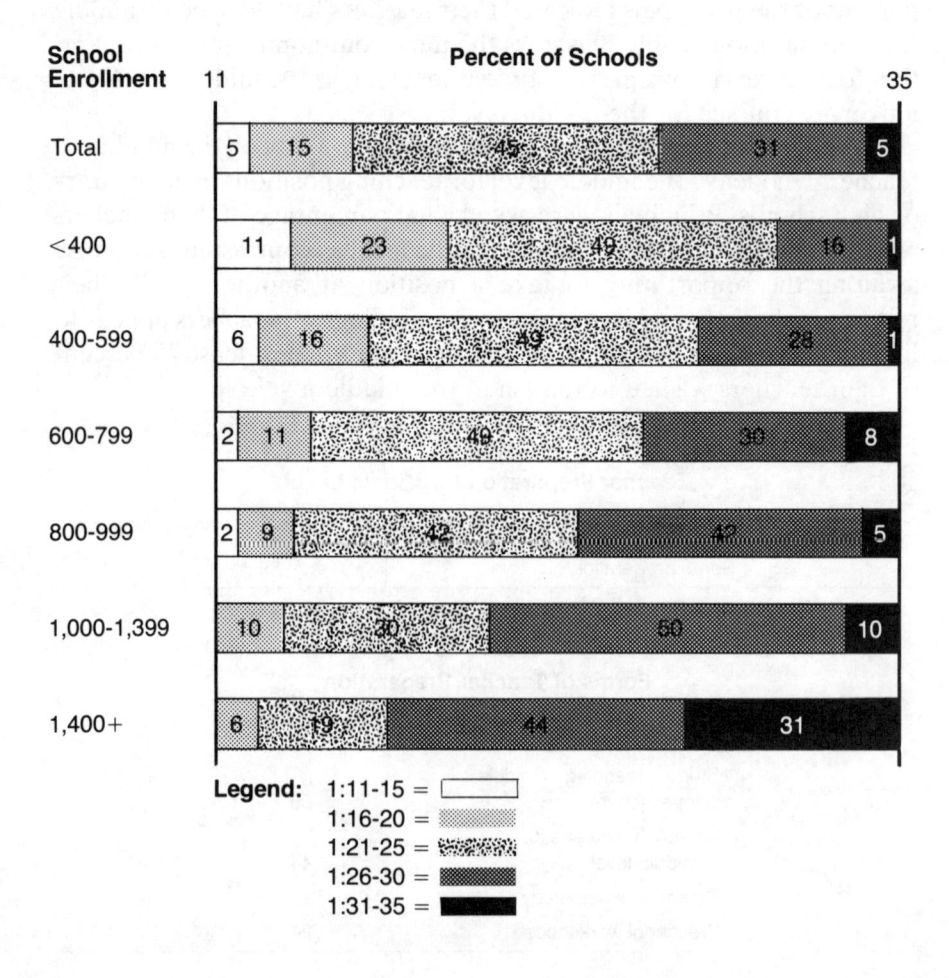

School Enrollment	Percent of Schools
	11 ... 35
Total	5 | 15 | 45 | 31 | 5
<400	11 | 23 | 49 | 16 | 1
400-599	6 | 16 | 49 | 28 | 1
600-799	2 | 11 | 49 | 30 | 8
800-999	2 | 9 | 42 | 42 | 5
1,000-1,399	10 | 30 | 50 | 10
1,400+	6 | 19 | 44 | 31

Legend:
1:11-15 =
1:16-20 =
1:21-25 =
1:26-30 =
1:31-35 =

TABLE 89
Teacher-Pupil Ratio by Enrollment

Ratio	Total	<400	400-599	600-799	800-999	1,000-1,399	1,400+
1:11-15	5	11	6	2	2	0	0
1:16-20	14	23	16	11	9	10	6
1:21-25	45	49	49	49	42	30	19
1:26-30	31	16	28	30	42	50	44
1:31-35	5	1	1	8	5	10	31

TABLE 90
Teacher-Pupil Ratio by Per-Pupil Expenditure

Ratio	Total	<$1,200	$1,200-1,799	$1,800+
1:11-15	5	3	4	7
1:16-20	14	9	14	26
1:21-25	45	43	49	38
1:26-30	31	37	29	26
1:31-35	5	8	4	0

TABLE 91
Enrollment Based upon Grade Level Configuration

	All Schools	7-8-9	7-8	6-7-8	5-6-7-8	Other
<400	20	8	31	19	44	26
400-599	25	19	30	30	30	25
600-799	24	27	24	24	13	28
800-999	18	26	9	18	9	14
1,000-1,399	10	15	6	8	4	6
1,400+	3	5	0	1	0	1

THE STUDENTS

Nearly 50 percent of middle level schools enroll between 400 and 800 students (Table 91). The median size is between 600 and 800. In 1966, the median junior high school size was 500-750 students. (The median senior high school size was 750-1,000 in 1978.) Schools of 7-8-9 grade levels were typically larger than schools of other grade level combinations. Schools of grades 5-6-7-8 were typically smaller. Middle level schools in rural areas were generally smaller than middle level schools in suburban and metropolitan areas.

Average Daily Attendance

Student average daily attendance (ADA) is especially important at the middle level. All students at that age are still under compulsory attendance laws. Their attendance in school is important not only to

TABLE 92
Average Daily Attendance by Grade Level

ADA	All Schools	Grade Level				Other
		7-8-9	7-8	6-7-8	5-6-7-8	
96+	19	13	25	27	29	9
91-95	60	62	58	59	65	64
81-90	18	21	15	12	6	26
<81	3	4	2	2	0	1

TABLE 93
Average Daily Attendance by Enrollment

ADA	All Schools	<400	400-599	600-799	800-999	1,000-1,399	1,400+
96+	19	31	18	20	12	12	5
91-95	60	56	59	65	63	61	47
81-90	18	10	20	14	23	23	24
<81	3	3	3	1	2	4	24

their personal growth and well-being but fiscally to districts and schools that receive financial support based upon daily attendance averages. Sixty percent of the principals indicated that their ADA was 91-95 percent. Table 92 indicates that schools with grades 7-8-9 had lower ADA than schools of 7-8, 6-7-8, and 5-6-7-8 patterns. The lowest ADA's by far were listed for schools of the "other" category. These were often single grade level schools. It might be appropriate to study single grade level schools further to determine if the pattern of attendance is consistent and, in some way, attributable to the single grade level arrangement.

Table 93 presents ADA analyzed on the basis of school enrollment. Smaller schools obviously have higher ADA records than the larger schools. This is especially noticeable in largest enrollment category (1,400 students or more) where nearly half the schools have ADA's at or below 90 percent.

THE COMMUNITY

The distribution of middle level schools in this study represents a cross section of the various communities throughout the nation. Table 94 shows the percentage of schools falling in each of the major population categories. The schools were also representative of the varied geographical regions of the country. Table 95 lists school breakdown by geographical region, the totals closely approximating the 1966 NASSP study.

FIGURE G (Based on Table 94)
Number of Schools by Community Population

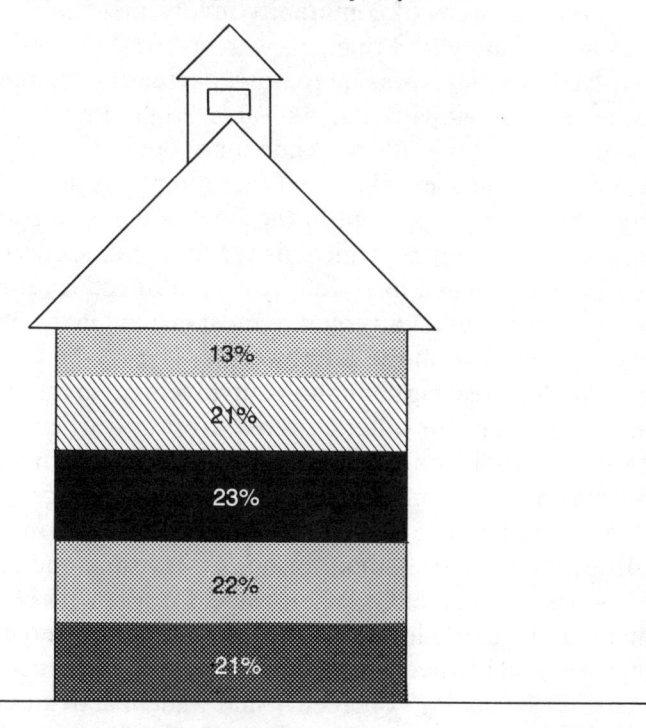

- 13%
- 21%
- 23%
- 22%
- 21%

CITY OF 150,000+ | SUBURBAN | 25,000-149,999 | 5,000-24,999 | RURAL

TABLE 94
Number of Schools by Community Population

	City of 150,000+	Suburban	25,000-149,999	5,000-24,999	Rural
Percent of Schools	13	21	23	22	21

TABLE 95
Number of Schools by Geographic Region

	New England	Middle Atlantic	South	Midwest	Southwest	Rocky Mountain	Far West
Percent of schools	8	15	18	33	9	5	12

Parental Participation in Schools

Several issues of community involvement in the educational process were examined. Principals were asked if the desire of parents to be involved in schools was increasing, decreasing, or remaining about the same as in previous years. As Table 96 points out, desire for involvement remains generally the same for about half of the schools reporting. More principals, however, feel that interest is increasing than decreasing. This is most apparent in the small towns and rural areas where 34 and 37 percent of the principals see parental desire for involvement on the increase. When analyzed by region of the country (Table 97), the desire for greater involvement is most evident in the New England states and least evident in the Southwest.

With increasing community involvement in the schools, the manner in which parents or other citizens currently participate in the *operation* of middle level schools is of interest. The most common forms of parent or citizen involvement are: 1. serving as resource persons in instructional programs (66 percent of the schools); 2. acting as volunteer aides (48 percent); and, 3. monitoring, supervising, and assisting at student activities (42 percent). When these forms of parent involvement are analyzed by grade level (Table 98) noteworthy percentages emerge for instructional involvement in 6-7-8 schools (75 percent), volunteer aides in 5-6-7-8 schools (71 percent), and student activities in 5-6-7-8 schools (57 percent.) Apparently, community involvement is somewhat more common in the 6-7-8 and 5-6-7-8 schools than in the other grade level configurations.

Ninety-two percent of the principals indicated that parents were involved in a *planning or advisory* capacity in their schools (Table 99). The most common forms of this involvement were in student activities (67 percent), developing objectives and priorities for the school (59 percent), program changes (59 percent), and student behavior, rights, and responsibilities (56 percent). It is interesting to note that 6-7-8 parents were most frequently involved in such areas of educational program development as objectives, priorities, and program change. Parents of 7-8-9 schools were more active in the areas of pupil personnel and student activities.

TABLE 96
Parent Involvement by Community Population

	All Schools	City of 150,000+	Suburban	25,000-149,999	5,000-24,999	Rural
Increasing	30	29	26	24	34	37
Decreasing	18	19	18	23	14	14
Same	52	52	56	53	52	49

TABLE 97
Parent Involvement by Geographic Region

	All Schools	New England	Middle Atlantic	South	Midwest	South-west	Rocky Mountain	Far West
Increasing	30	41	27	33	30	24	30	29
Decreasing	18	14	19	21	17	13	14	19
Same	52	45	54	46	53	63	56	52

TABLE 98
Parent/Citizen Involvement in School Operation by Grade Level

	All Schools	7-8-9	7-8	6-7-8	5-6-7-8	Other
Resource persons in instructional program	66	65	68	75	54	60
Volunteer aides	48	46	50	49	71	44
Monitor, supervise, sell tickets at student activities	42	41	43	43	57	32

TABLE 99
Parent Involvement in Planning/Advisory Capacity by Grade Level

	All Schools	7-8-9	7-8	6-7-8	5-6-7-8	Other
Objectives/Priorities	59	59	62	64	38	56
Program change	59	61	58	60	48	53
Student activities	67	68	65	72	43	64
Student behavior, rights, responsibilities	56	59	55	55	33	49

Community Pressure Groups

In recent years, the impact of pressure groups on schools has received increasing publicity. The principals in the study were asked about the degree to which selected community forces influenced their schools. Local elementary and high schools, teacher associations, and PTA/PTOs had the greatest overall influence. Groups that principals felt generally had little or no influence were left/right wing extremists, local labor organizations, legal aid groups, and censorship groups. Table 100 lists some of the more common community pressure groups and the types of communities where these groups have the most and/or least influence. Generally speaking, metropolitan areas were most affected by pressure groups; suburban and rural areas the least.

FIGURE H (Based on Table 100)
Community Pressure Groups by Population

TYPE OF COMMUNITY

	RURAL	SUBURBAN	5,000-24,999	25,000-149,999	City of 150,000+
Censorship	★	☆			
Groups Concerned About National Studies	☆				★
Left/Right Wing Extremists	☆	☆	★		
Local Media	☆	☆			★
PTA/PTO				☆	★
Religious Groups	★	☆			★
Teacher Associations				★	
Women's Organizations	☆				★

★ MOST INFLUENCE   ☆ LEAST INFLUENCE

TABLE 100
Community Pressure Groups by Population

	Type of Community	
Group	Most Influence	Least Influence
Censorship	Rural	Suburban
Groups concerned about national studies	150,000+	Rural
Left/Right wing extremists	5,000-24,999	Suburban/Rural
Local media	150,000+	Suburban/Rural
PTA/PTO	150,000+	<25,000
Religious groups	150,000+/Rural	Suburban
Teacher associations	<25,000	<25,000
Women's organizations	150,000+	Rural

Summary

In this chapter questions related to staff, students, and community were presented.

Size and diversity of staff have increased noticeably in recent years. Women form the majority of the middle level teaching staff in contrast with a significantly disproportionate percentage of male administrators. Teacher preparation for the middle level has apparently made some progress in recent years; but nearly half of the principals note that their faculty members still have had no specific training for teaching at this level. Despite some shortcomings, most middle level teachers desire to remain at this level.

Teacher-pupil ratios varied widely by school size and per-pupil expenditure. Smaller schools and those spending more money had lower ratios.

Average daily attendance reflected school size and grade organization. Smaller schools and grade 5-6-7-8 schools had better attendance records.

Median school size was 600-800 students. Grade 7-8-9 schools were larger; 5-6-7-8 schools smaller.

Principals of many communities, in particular small towns and rural areas, are observing an increase in parental desire for involvement in the schools. Interestingly, these same small town/rural areas remain least affected by community pressure groups.

IV School Programs

This chapter presents the data gathered on middle level school programs. For reporting purposes the chapter is divided into organizational and instructional subsections.

SCHOOL ORGANIZATION

Type of School

Principals participating in this study administered three distinct types of schools: public, parochial or diocesan, and private, religious affiliated. There were no respondents from private, nonreligious schools. Ninety-eight percent of the principals were from public schools. Administrators from parochial/diocesan and private religious-affiliated schools each represented 1 percent of the sample.

Grade level organization (Table 101) showed that 43 percent of the public schools included grades 7-8-9, while the most popular pattern for religious-affiliated schools was the 7-8 configuration. It is interesting to note that 36 percent of the parochial and 28 percent of the private religious schools were organized with 5-6-7-8 or 6-7-8 grade levels. Only 19 percent of the public schools in this study had these grade level organizational patterns.

When the data were examined by region it was found that parochial schools were most prevalent in New England (27 percent) and in the Midwest (27 percent). Private schools with religious affiliation were most numerous in the South (43 percent) and the Middle Atlantic region (29 percent).

Important size differences are evident in Table 102 for the three types of schools. Fifty percent of the public schools enrolled between

TABLE 101
Grade Level by Type of School

	Total	Public	Parochial	Private Religious
7-8-9	42	43	18	—
7-8	31	31	45	43
6-7-8	15	15	18	14
5-6-7-8	4	4	18	14
Other	8	7	1	29

TABLE 102
Type of School by Enrollment

	Public	Parochial	Private Religious
<400	19	73	86
400-599	25	18	14
600-799	24	9	—
800-999	18	—	—
1,000-1,399	10	—	—
1,400+	3	—	—

400 and 800 pupils. Parochial schools had enrollments of 600 or less in 91 percent of the cases, and all of the private schools indicated enrollments of less than 600.

Grade Level Organization

The most common grade level organization in NASSP's 1980 study was 7-8-9, with 42 percent of the principals reporting that grade level structure. The 7-8 grade level organization was represented by 31 percent of the administrators. The typical "middle school" grade level groupings of 6-7-8 and 5-6-7-8 showed 15 and 4 percent, respectively.

Data in Table 103 show that the highest incidence *across* regions of all the different grade level combinations was reported in the Midwest—almost half of the 5-6-7-8 schools of the study were located in that region. Virtually one-half of the nontypical configurations ("Other") were reported in the South. Examination of grade level organization *within* regions (Table 104) indicates that 7-8-9 and 7-8 configurations dominated the Rocky Mountain region (90 percent) and the Far West (89 percent). The Southwest, with 30 percent, and New England, with 24 percent, seem to favor the typical middle school combinations of 6-7-8 and 5-6-7-8.

Grade level data when analyzed by population show that the 7-8-9 school most frequently was located in population areas that exceeded 25,000. A higher percentage of 6-7-8 and 5-6-7-8 schools were located

TABLE 103
Grade Level Across Regions

	7-8-9	7-8	6-7-8	5-6-7-8	Other
New England	6	11	11	11	6
Middle Atlantic	18	11	15	11	11
South	16	12	23	12	48
Midwest	33	35	27	46	21
Southwest	6	10	16	11	8
Rocky Mountain	8	3	1	2	2
Far West	13	18	7	7	4

TABLE 104
Grade Level Within Regions

	Total	New England	Middle Atlantic	South	Midwest	Southwest	Rocky Mountain	Far West
7-8-9	42	33	52	38	43	28	71	42
7-8	31	39	24	21	34	34	19	47
6-7-8	15	18	15	19	12	25	3	4
5-6-7-8	4	6	3	2	6	5	1	1
Other	8	4	6	20	5	8	6	6

in population areas of less than 25,000. Over half (57 percent) of the 5-6-7-8 schools were located in rural areas.

Data on the relationship of grade level organization to enrollment show that 7-8-9 schools tended to be larger than schools with 7-8, 6-7-8, or 5-6-7-8 configurations. Almost two-thirds of the 7-8 and 6-7-8 schools reported that their enrollments were in the 400-799 range. Three-quarters of the 5-6-7-8 schools had enrollments of 599 or less.

Status of Grade Level Patterns

The data in Table 105 outline the historical status of grade level patterns in middle level schools. Almost one-fifth of all the schools in the study have been in their current grade level organization 5 years or less. Sixty-five percent of 5-6-7-8 schools and 61 percent of 6-7-8 schools have employed their current organization for 10 years or less. A majority (51 percent) of the 7-8 schools have changed grade levels within the last 10 years. Conversely, over one-third of 7-8-9 schools have remained unchanged for 21 or more years.

Regional data show the majority of the schools in New England (55 percent), the South (63 percent), and the Southwest (60 percent) with grade level changes in the last 10 years. The Rocky Mountain and Far West regions have remained much more stable.

Population data indicate that 35-40 percent of schools in intermediate to large cities have not changed grade level organization in over

TABLE 105
Years Using the Current Organizational Pattern by Grade Level

	Total	7-8-9	7-8	6-7-8	5-6-7-8	Other
<5 years	19	11	21	32	25	32
6-10 years	26	18	30	29	40	41
11-15 years	19	20	14	26	20	25
16-20 years	14	15	20	10	5	—
21 years+	22	36	15	3	10	2

21 years. Less densely populated areas appear to be more prone to change. Half of the schools located in small and rural communities have changed within the last 10 years.

Change to Middle School Configurations

Reasons given for change to a 5-6-7-8 or 6-7-8 organizational pattern by the 25 percent of respondents who reported change are summarized in Table 106. This table also gives comparative data collected by Brooks (1977) and Alexander (1967). The comparisons show that enrollment shift is now perceived less often as a reason for changing to 5-6-7-8 or 6-7-8 grade level organizations. The current NASSP study (1980) and the Brooks study establish that curriculum and student articulation concerns are the most frequently cited reasons for adopting middle school grade level organization.

Per-Pupil Expenditure

The per-pupil expenditures for the 1979-1980 school year are presented in Table 107. Principals of all but 5-6-7-8 schools indicated that their typical per-pupil expenditure was in the midrange of $1,200-1,799. The highest percentage of principals in 5-6-7-8 schools reported per-pupil expenditures of $1,199 or less. They also reported the highest percentage of expenditures of $1,800 or more.

Regional data showed approximately half of the New England and Far West schools in the lowest per-pupil expenditure range. The Southwest and the Rocky Mountain regions had the smallest percentage of schools in that range. The Southwest, Rocky Mountain, and Middle Atlantic regions reported that more than one-fifth of their schools spent more than $1,800 per pupil.

TABLE 106
Reasons for Change to 5-6-7-8 or 6-7-8 Configuration

NASSP	Brooks	Alexander	
61	68	45	Provide program suited to middle level child.
57	63	40	Provide better transition from elementary to high school.
46	48	58	Adjust to enrollment trends.
31	23	24	Employ new curricular/instructional innovations.
28	18	20	Utilize new school facility/building.
26	20	30	Provide 5th or 6th graders with more curricular specialization.
24	36	25	Solve concerns about junior high program.
19	29	25	Move ninth graders into high school program.
17	13	13	Employ ideas/programs successfully implemented in other schools.

**FIGURE I (Based on Table 106)
Reasons for Change to 5-6-7-8 or 6-7-8 Configuration**

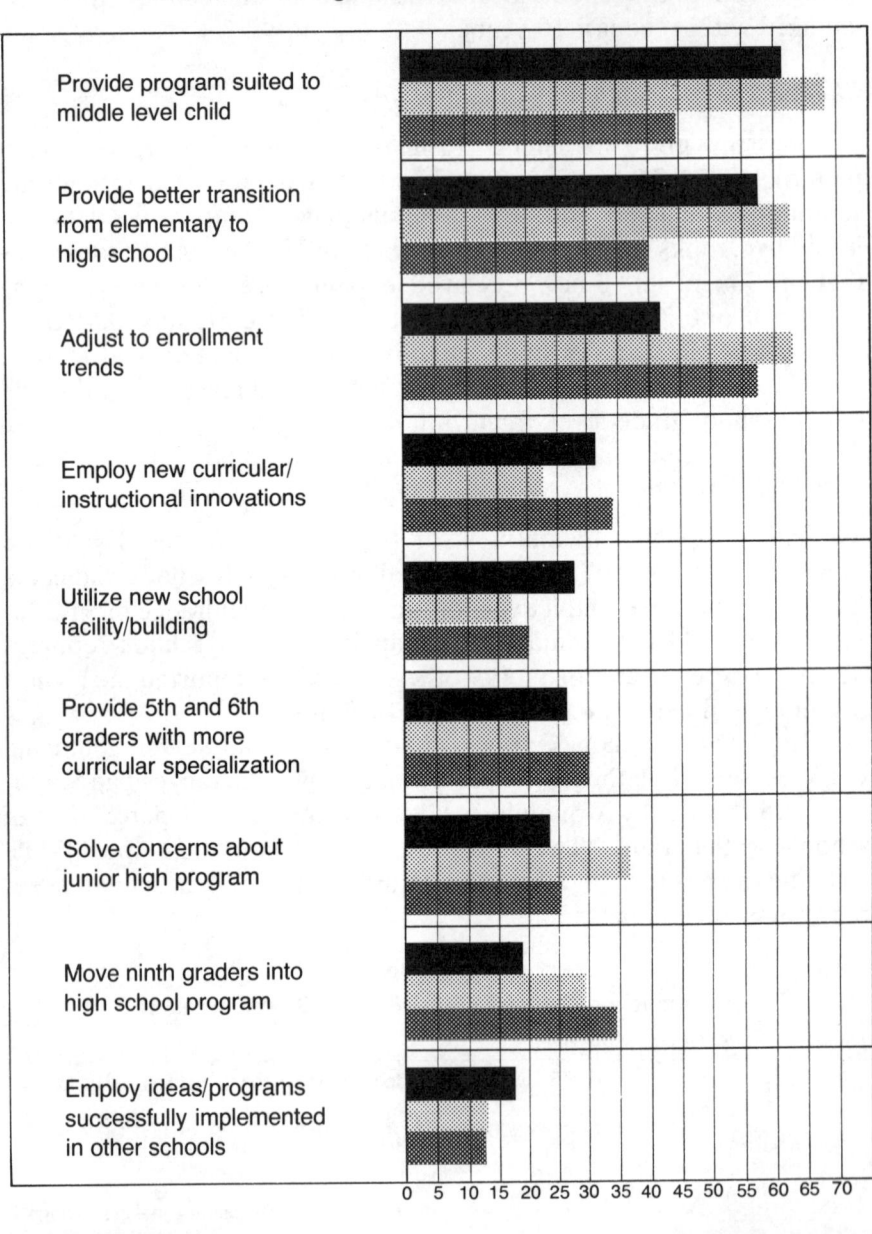

Provide program suited to middle level child	
Provide better transition from elementary to high school	
Adjust to enrollment trends	
Employ new curricular/instructional innovations	
Utilize new school facility/building	
Provide 5th and 6th graders with more curricular specialization	
Solve concerns about junior high program	
Move ninth graders into high school program	
Employ ideas/programs successfully implemented in other schools	

Scale: 0 5 10 15 20 25 30 35 40 45 50 55 60 65 70

Legend: NASSP—1980, Brooks—1977, Alexander—1967

One-third of the suburban schools indicated that they spent more than $1,800 per year per student. All other population areas showed a lower pattern of spending.

Types of Facilities

A majority of school principals indicated that the following types of facilities were available in their schools:

- Gymnasium
- Library
- Instructional materials center
- Media center
- Industrial arts lab
- Reading lab
- Music room
- Art room

The data in Table 108 reflect very few differences in the types of facilities found in the four different grade level organizations.

TABLE 107
Average Per-Pupil Expenditure by Grade Level

	Total	7-8-9	7-8	6-7-8	5-6-7-8	Other
<$1,200	38	35	36	40	40	44
$1,200-1,799	43	45	45	44	36	46
$1,800+	19	20	19	16	24	10

TABLE 108
Types of Facilities by Grade Level

	Total	7-8-9	7-8	6-7-8	5-6-7-8	Other
Gymnasium	89	90	88	90	88	83
Library	91	90	93	96	91	86
Instructional materials center	53	52	52	56	54	58
Media center	53	58	45	53	43	60
Industrial arts lab	79	85	76	80	57	64
Mathematics lab	34	36	37	31	17	30
Reading lab	64	67	65	64	43	58
Social science lab	15	15	18	16	9	14
Language lab	28	33	21	25	14	38
Music room	91	92	90	95	85	83
Art room	87	91	88	87	80	70
Crafts room	45	49	45	43	25	42
Computer or data processing facility	21	27	20	17	14	11

Cross comparisons of the six types of facilities listed in the 1966 NASSP study with current equivalents (Table 109) show a considerable improvement in the types of middle level facilities available. With the exception of language labs (moderate decrease) and industrial arts labs (moderate increase), the data indicate significant increases in the percentages of schools with gymnasiums, libraries, and music and art rooms.

Types of facilities were also examined by region, population, enrollment, and per-pupil expenditure. In most cases, few differences were found. Gymnasiums exist in only two-thirds of the Far West schools (the weather is a factor) compared to Midwest schools where 96 percent reported having gymnasiums. Craft rooms were more common in Rocky Mountain and Far West schools and less common in New England schools. Rural areas were less likely to have media centers, reading labs, industrial arts labs, language labs, and arts and crafts facilities. Greater school enrollment was related to the availability of four types of facilities: math labs, and music, art, and crafts rooms. Schools with per-pupil expenditures over $1,800 reported higher incidence of industrial arts labs, instructional material centers, and math labs.

INSTRUCTIONAL PROGRAM

The various patterns of instructional program organization to be examined include instructional formats, subject organizational patterns, required and elective courses, supplementary programs, ability grouping, and programs for the gifted. Also included are data on sports and student activities, school articulation, accreditation, parent conferences, and use of data processing.

Instructional Formats

Principals were asked to estimate the percent of time students at each grade level spent in the instructional formats of traditional classroom (15-35 students), small group instruction (2-15 students), large

TABLE 109
Comparison of Types of Facilities

	NASSP 1980	NASSP 1966
Gymnasium	89	77
Library	91	79
Industrial arts lab	79	72
Language lab	28	30
Music room	91	75
Art room	87	68

TABLE 110
Instructional Organization by Grade Level

Organizational Format	Grades				
	5	6	7	8	9
Traditional class size (15-35 students)	1	1	1	1	1
Small group instruction (2-15 students)	2	2	2	2	2
Large group instruction (More than 35 students)	3.5	3.5	3.5	3.5	3.5
Individualized instruction	3.5	3.5	3.5	3.5	3.5

group instruction (more than 35 students), and individualized instruction. Table 110 gives the rank order of time typically spent by students in the four instructional formats. The rank order reflects median percentages for the four formats, scaled from 1 (highest) to 4.

Students in middle level schools spend most of their instructional time in traditional class size formats. In all graded schools, the traditional classroom was the instructional organization that received the highest ranking. Large group and individualized instruction were the least used formats in all schools. The small group format made its strongest showing in nongraded schools (reported by only 1.4 percent of the schools).

When comparisons were made with the Brooks and the Alexander studies, it was evident that very little change had taken place. Middle level education is still predominantly a traditional classroom operation.

Subject Patterns

Principals were asked to judge the amount of time that students spend in each of four subject matter instructional patterns:

A. One subject taught by one teacher
B. Several subjects taught by one teacher
C. Single subject area teams
D. Several subjects with interdisciplinary teams

Items are ranked in Table 111 according to median percentages that represent, at that grade level, the formats listed.

The subject specialist instructional format is the preferred choice at all but the fifth grade level. The self-contained approach was used most frequently at the lower grade levels. Interdisciplinary teaming appeared to be somewhat more popular than the single subject area team approach.

TABLE 111
Subject Organization for Instruction

Instructional Format	Grades				
	5	6	7	8	9
A. One subject taught by one teacher (subject specialist).	3.5	1	1	1	1
B. Several subjects taught by one teacher (self-contained).	1	2	3.5	3	4
C. One subject taught by team (subject area team).	3.5	4	3.5	3	3
D. Several subjects taught by team (interdisciplinary team).	2	3	2	3	2

Required and Elective Courses

To determine the typical courses of study offered in middle level schools, principals were asked to check a listing of courses and indicate by grade level (1) those that were required in their schools, and (2) those that were available as electives. Table 112 presents the data by grade level. Several trends seem apparent:

- The five subjects of English/language arts, math, science, social studies, and physical education are almost universally required of all students at all grade levels. These five subjects recorded percentages of 90 or above from all respondents.
- Reading as a requirement received high percentages at the fifth (98 percent) and sixth (95 percent) grade levels. At the seventh, eighth, and ninth grades, it fell to 72, 60, and 26 percent respectively.
- Across all grade levels, instrumental music was the most popular elective offered. At grades 7, 8, and 9, art and vocal music were highly rated electives, but at the fifth and sixth grade levels they tended to be requirements rather than electives.

The 6-7-8 and 5-6-7-8 schools tended to have more requirements and fewer electives than the 7-8-9 and 7-8 schools. The 7-8-9 buildings offered the most electives and these choices were not confined solely to ninth grade. Seventh and eighth graders in 7-8-9 schools appeared to have far more course options than seventh and eighth graders in 5-6-7-8 schools. Seventh and eighth graders in the 6-7-8 and 7-8 schools, however, seemed to have opportunities similar to their counterparts in 7-8-9 schools.

The data also showed that sixth graders in 6-7-8 grade schools and fifth and sixth graders in 5-6-7-8 grade schools took mostly required

TABLE 112
Required Courses and Electives

Content Area	5 R	5 E	6 R	6 E	7 R	7 E	8 R	8 E	9 R	9 E
English/Language arts	100	0	100	0	99	1	98	2	96	4
Math	100	0	100	0	99	1	98	2	92	8
Science	100	0	99	1	93	3	93	5	72	25
Social studies	93	0	97	0	96	1	93	3	80	17
Reading	98	0	95	1	72	17	60	22	26	33
Physical ed.	95	2	99	1	96	4	91	8	86	14
Health	68	2	76	1	64	3	55	5	37	9
Home economics	12	2	31	10	46	30	42	49	15	91
Industrial arts	10	5	30	11	43	31	42	48	15	90
Art	66	2	64	15	52	38	37	55	13	86
Crafts	7	2	11	11	11	22	10	30	5	48
General music	56	2	61	13	50	22	30	23	8	27
Vocal music	27	5	17	19	14	41	1	48	7	63
Instrum. music	10	34	13	67	15	82	11	84	8	91
Orchestra	—	4	—	22	—	42	—	44	5	57
Foreign language	5	2	8	8	7	36	9	48	11	82
Typing	—	2	—	6	4	13	6	25	6	56
Speech	5	0	9	4	7	15	7	23	7	40
Drama	—	10	—	13	—	20	—	30	2	42
Photography	—	2	—	8	—	11	—	15	2	23
Career education	10	0	17	3	26	10	27	12	19	25
Spelling	98	0	85	0	64	1	58	2	36	1
Chorus	0	10	0	33	0	58	0	68	7	83

R = Required, E = Elective

courses. Ninty-five percent or more of the schools with those two grade levels indicated that English/language arts, mathematics, science, social studies, reading, and physical education were requirements. With the exception of instrumental music, fifth and sixth graders were provided few electives.

The findings of this survey were similar to those of the Brooks study in which middle school administrators reported basically the same requirements for English/language arts, mathematics, science, social studies, reading, and physical education. Brooks also found that 95 percent of the 5-6-7-8 and 6-7-8 had a spelling requirement. The current NASSP survey revealed that in 5-6-7-8 schools, 100 percent of the fifth and sixth graders, 81 percent of the seventh graders, and 67 percent of the eighth graders were required to take spelling. In 6-7-8 schools, the percentage requiring spelling ranged from 82 percent at the sixth grade level to 64 percent at the eighth grade level. In 7-8 schools, spelling was required by 72 percent of the schools for seventh graders and by 68 percent of the schools for eighth graders. Spelling requirements in 7-8-9 schools ranged from 54 percent for seventh graders to 38 percent for ninth graders. It is clear that there is a tendency to drop spelling as a requirement at the higher grade levels.

Types of Supplementary Programs

Many schools offered opportunities for students to obtain instruction over and above the regular school program. When principals were asked to summarize the types of optional programs that were available to students in their schools, summer school was the only one selected by a majority (Table 113). Opportunity to attend summer school ranged from 63 percent in 7-8-9 schools to 31 percent in 5-6-7-8 schools. Enrollment in high school courses was listed as an available option by 35 percent of the administrators, but was most common in 7-8-9 schools (43 percent). All other discretionary programs were available in less than 15 percent of the schools.

The data in Table 114 show that summer school is more available in the more populated areas, with a range of 60 to 67 percent, dropping to only 27 percent in rural areas. The latter, however, made high school courses available more often (36 percent) than any of the other areas, suburban alone excepting.

School enrollment was also a factor influencing the type of programs available to students. Table 115 verifies that larger schools,

TABLE 113
Types of Programs for Which Students May Enroll by Grade Level Organization

	Total	7-8-9	7-8	6-7-8	5-6-7-8	Other
High school courses	35	43	28	27	37	29
Credit by exam	6	6	4	4	6	11
Credit by contract	14	15	13	12	9	12
Off-campus work	11	18	4	12	6	6
Community volunteer	10	12	9	10	3	5
Summer school	52	63	41	54	31	55

TABLE 114
Types of Programs for Which Students May Enroll by Population

	City of 150,000+	Suburban	25,000-149,999	5,000-24,999	Rural
High school courses	32	41	31	35	36
Credit by examination	12	7	3	3	5
Credit by contract	14	15	14	14	12
Off-campus work experience	12	15	13	11	5
Community volunteer programs	15	15	9	7	5
Summer school	60	60	67	46	27
Other	2	8	3	2	8

particularly those falling in 1,000-1,399 range, tended to offer more opportunities for off-campus work experience. Almost one-fourth of the schools over 1,400 offered a credit by contract option. The larger the enrollment, the greater the percentage of schools with a summer school option. The latter ranged from 31 percent for schools of 400 or less to 76 percent for schools with enrollments of 1,400 or more.

Ability Grouping

Two items in this survey dealt with ability grouping. The extent to which ability grouping was used in middle level schools and the criteria employed for grouping were the focus of the first question. A second question sought to determine the scope of existing policies for such grouping.

Generally speaking, existing research fails to justify the use of ability grouping in schools apart from specialized programs for the gifted and/or disabled. In this light, it is amazing that 88 percent of the schools in this study reported they were using some form of ability grouping (Table 116). Very few differences were found among the four grade level organizations. Ability grouping was most common in 7-8-9 and 6-7-8 schools (89 percent) and least common in 5-6-7-8 schools (80 percent).

TABLE 115
Types of Programs for Which Students May Enroll by Enrollment

	<400	400-599	600-799	800-999	1,000-1,399	1,400+
High school courses	35	31	37	43	27	29
Credit by examination	5	3	5	7	9	18
Credit by contract	14	9	16	19	9	24
Off-campus work experience	6	9	8	16	23	18
Community volunteer programs	7	11	11	7	15	12
Summer school	31	51	56	63	64	76
Other	8	5	3	5	1	0

TABLE 116
Ability Grouping by Grade Level Organization

	Total	7-8-9	7-8	6-7-8	5-6-7-8	Other
No ability grouping	12	11	14	11	20	18
Ability grouping	88	89	86	89	80	82

FIGURE J (Based on Table 116)
Ability Grouping by Grade Level Organization

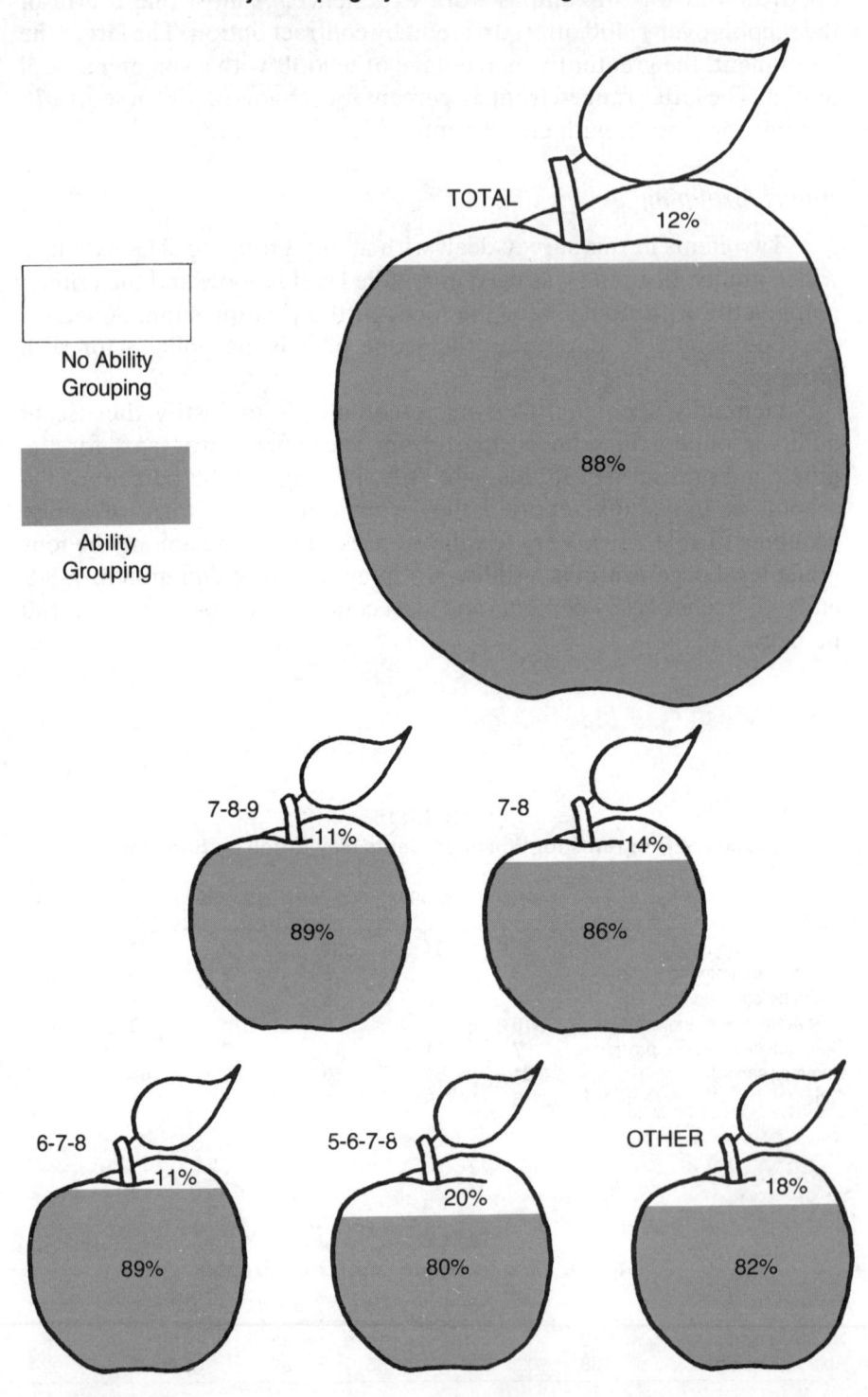

No Ability Grouping

Ability Grouping

TOTAL — 12% / 88%

7-8-9 — 11% / 89%

7-8 — 14% / 86%

6-7-8 — 11% / 89%

5-6-7-8 — 20% / 80%

OTHER — 18% / 82%

68

Staff judgments and standardized tests were the most frequently cited methods for making decisions about student placement. Grades also were perceived as an important criterion for grouping. Schools with 6-7-8 grades placed the highest value on standardized tests (92 percent) while 5-6-7-8 schools favored them the least (71 percent). The latter (5-6-7-8) also employed parental input markedly less than schools with the other grade level formats.

Population and enrollment seemed to have little influence on ability grouping and its placement criteria, although rural and small schools did report lesser use of the practice.

In schools with ability grouping practices, principals were asked to indicate the scope of the grouping policies. Two-thirds of the principals reported that grouping took place at "all grade levels but only in certain subjects" (Table 118). Grouping at all grade levels in all subjects (commonly called tracking) existed in only 10 percent of all schools but in 20 percent of 6-7-8 schools.

TABLE 117
Criteria for Grouping Students by Grade Level Organization

	Total	7-8-9	7-8	6-7-8	5-6-7-8	Other
Grades	69	75	64	66	46	67
I.Q. scores	41	42	40	38	35	35
Staff judgments	85	86	84	87	71	81
Standardized tests	83	81	81	92	71	83
Parental input	43	47	40	43	21	52
Criterion-referenced tests	46	46	47	46	36	43
Other	4	4	4	2	7	7

TABLE 118
Scope of Ability Grouping by Grade Level Organization

	Total	7-8-9	7-8	6-7-8	5-6-7-8	Other
Grouping—All grade levels, all subjects	10	7	8	20	6	13
Grouping—All grade levels, certain subjects	67	65	74	59	63	59
Grouping—Certain grade levels, all subjects	2	1	1	6	6	4
Grouping—Certain grade levels, certain subjects	17	23	13	11	25	11
Different grouping systems	4	4	4	5	0	7

TABLE 119
Comparison of Grouping Policies
NASSP 1980 and NASSP 1966

	NASSP 1980	NASSP 1966
Grouping—All grade levels, all subjects	9	15
Grouping—All grade levels, certain subjects	59	53
Grouping—Certain grade levels, all subjects	2	5
Grouping—Certain grade levels, certain subjects	15	15
No ability grouping	11	9
Other	4	3

Population influenced ability grouping to the extent that the percentage of schools reporting grouping in all grades and in certain subjects increased from 59 percent in rural areas to a high of 76 percent in metropolitan areas with populations of 150,000 or more. School size was also an influencing factor. The smaller the school, the more varied the grouping practices.

Data in Table 119 compare current grouping practices with those reported in 1966. There have been few changes. It is encouraging that tracking has decreased but it appears that the principles and practice of traditional ability grouping have maintained their popularity in middle level schools.

Programs for the Gifted

When administrators were asked about gifted programs in their schools, 30 percent said that they had none. Those who responded affirmatively, however, were asked to indicate criteria for admittance to the programs and to describe their organizational formats (Tables 120 and 121).

Approximately 70 percent of 7-8-9, 7-8, and 6-7-8 schools reported gifted programs; but only about half (52 percent) of the 5-6-7-8 schools indicated that they had programs.

School size appeared to be a factor in the establishment of gifted programs. Only 57 percent of schools with enrollments of 400 or less reported the existence of programs, while more than three-quarters of the schools with enrollments of 800 or more did so. Since 5-6-7-8 schools are smaller on the average than other middle level configurations, the lower incidence of gifted programs in these schools may simply be a result of their size.

Per-pupil expenditure was not a factor in school grouping practices.

FIGURE K (Based on Table 120)
Gifted Programs by Grade Level Organization

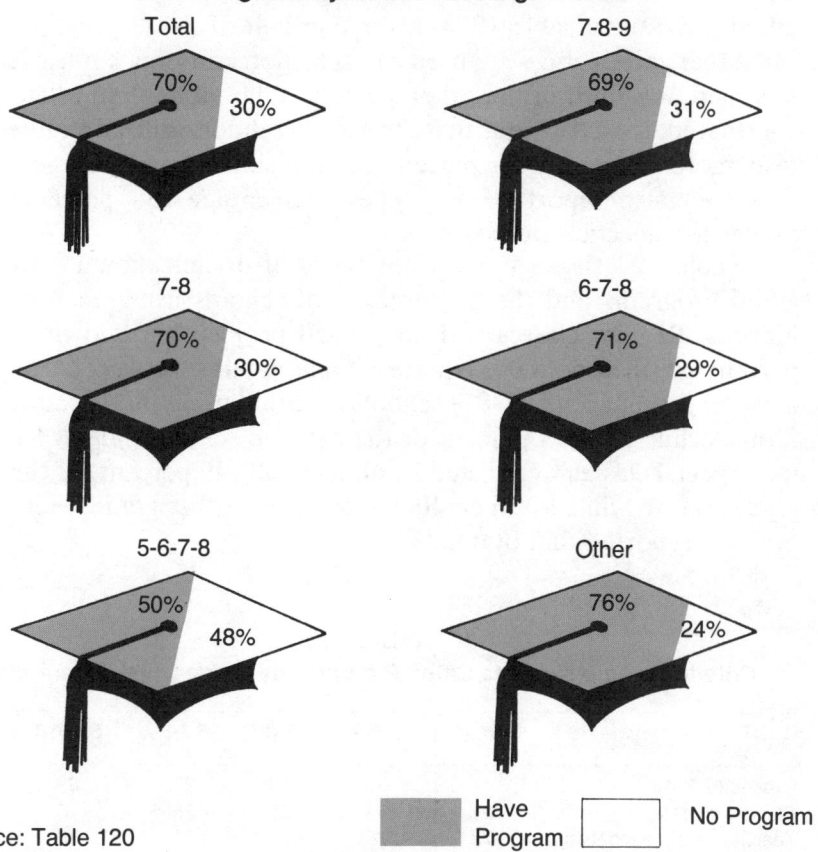

- Total: 70% Have Program, 30% No Program
- 7-8-9: 69% Have Program, 31% No Program
- 7-8: 70% Have Program, 30% No Program
- 6-7-8: 71% Have Program, 29% No Program
- 5-6-7-8: 50% Have Program, 48% No Program
- Other: 76% Have Program, 24% No Program

Source: Table 120

TABLE 120
Gifted Programs by Grade Level Organization

	Total	7-8-9	7-8	6-7-8	5-6-7-8	Other
No Program	30	31	30	29	48	24
Have Program	70	69	70	71	52	76

TABLE 121
Criteria for Admittance to Gifted Programs by Enrollment

	<400	400-599	600-799	800-999	1,000-1,399	1,400+
No program	43	34	26	20	18	20
Have program	57	66	74	80	82	80
Criteria						
Grades (G.P.A.)	43	35	38	45	41	54
Student interest	33	31	28	33	28	38
Teacher recommendation	74	72	75	75	66	77
Standardized tests	72	72	80	77	83	92
Other	21	16	16	20	17	15

In all schools, standardized tests and teacher recommendations were the two most frequently reported criteria for placing students in gifted programs (Table 122). Over one-half of 7-8-9 principals indicated that grades also were used as a selection criterion, contrasted with less than one-third in the other schools. When school enrollment was considered, it was obvious that the largest schools utilized standardized tests more frequently for placement than smaller ones. Large schools (1,400+) also reported the highest percentage (54 percent) using grades for selection purposes.

Table 123 shows the various types of organizational format for gifted programs and the percentages of schools using each of these formats. Regular classes with individual projects showed the highest percentage of response (51 percent) among all schools reporting. Almost 60 percent of the 7-8-9 schools reported using this organizational format while only 35 percent of the 5-6-7-8 schools did so. Released time special classes were listed by almost half (49 percent) of the 6-7-8 grade schools while less than 40 percent of the other grade level configurations reported that option.

TABLE 122
Criteria for Admittance to Gifted Programs by Grade Level Organization

	Total	7-8-9	7-8	6-7-8	5-6-7-8	Other
Grades (G.P.A.)	41	53	29	27	27	38
Student interest	31	35	28	26	0	29
Teacher recommendation	73	78	69	61	73	74
Standardized tests	77	82	70	77	73	76
Other	18	15	16	26	9	18

TABLE 123
Organizational Format for Gifted Programs by Grade Level Organization

	Total	7-8-9	7-8	6-7-8	5-6-7-8	Other
Released time for special classes	38	34	35	49	38	44
Regular class with individual projects	51	59	48	45	35	42
After school, evening, weekend programs	13	13	15	10	4	13
Summer program	9	11	9	10	4	6
Co-op program with high school	8	4	12	8	9	8
Program in conjunction with district, region, or state	15	15	14	18	9	17
Other	8	9	8	7	4	2

FIGURE L (Based on Table 123)
Organizational Format for Gifted Programs by Grade Level Organization

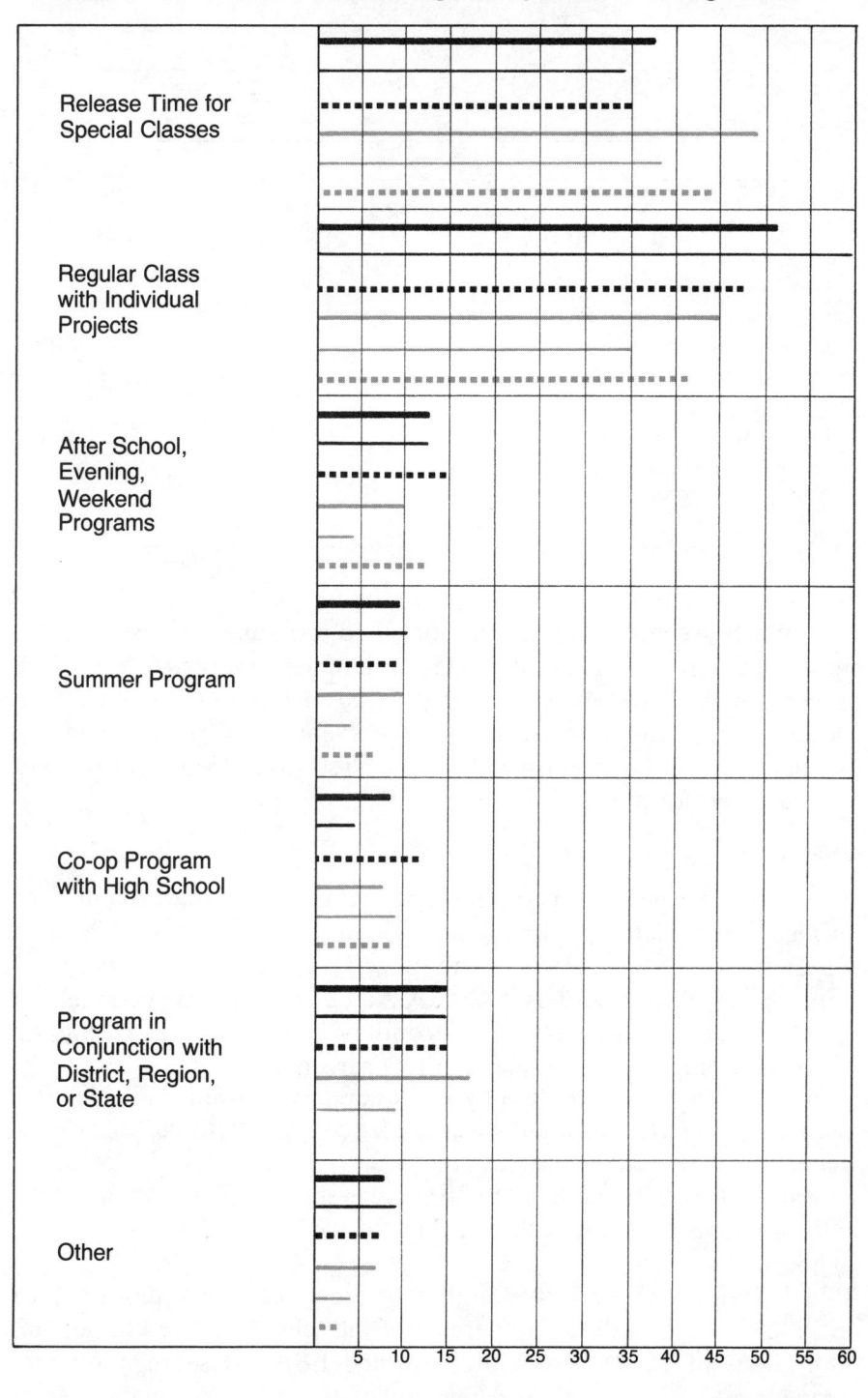

Legend	
——— Total	——— 6-7-8
——— 7-8-9	——— 5-6-7-8
▪▪▪▪▪ 7-8	▪▪▪▪▪ Other

TABLE 124
Organizational Format for Gifted Programs by Per-Pupil Expenditure

	<$1,200	$1,200-1,799	$1,800+
No program	33	34	40
Have program	67	66	60
Organization			
Released time for special classes	41	36	40
Regular class with individual projects	50	57	47
After school, evening, or weekend programs	9	16	19
Summer programs	5	12	12
Co-op program with high school	5	9	13
Program in conjunction with district, region, or state	16	19	9
Other	8	6	12

When organizational format for gifted programs was examined in terms of per-pupil expenditure, a few differences emerged (Table 124). Schools with higher expenditures ($1,200+) reported a higher incidence of programs after school, in the evening, or on weekends, in summer, and in cooperation with local high schools. Availability of staff may account for much of this differential.

State and Federally-Funded Programs

All but 2 percent of the respondents indicated that they had received special state or federal funding in the past three years. The most frequently cited programs were Special Education (77 percent), Emergency School Aid Act (E.S.A.A.) Title IV—Instructional (64 percent), and Elementary and Secondary Education Act (E.S.E.A.) Title I—Compensatory Education (63 percent).

Examination of the data by grade level organization (Table 125) showed that Title I programs were most commonly found in 5-6-7-8 schools (79 percent) and least often in 7-8-9 schools (58 percent). Vocational education funded programs were found in almost half of the 7-8-9 schools and in less than a third of the 7-8, 6-7-8, and 5-6-7-8 schools.

Rural areas had the highest percentage (83 percent) of ESEA—Title I funds. Forty percent of the schools located in population areas of 150,000 or more reported ESAA-desegregation programs while no more than 6 percent of the other population areas

TABLE 125
Funded Programs by Grade Level Organization

	Total	7-8-9	7-8	6-7-8	5-6-7-8	Other
No federal or state funding	2	2	2	1	3	0
Funded programs	98	98	98	99	97	100
Type of Programs						
Federal Title I—ESEA	63	58	62	71	79	71
State Compensatory Education	23	21	21	30	23	27
Vocational Education	38	48	29	30	26	44
Impact Aid	22	27	17	21	6	32
Career Education	33	34	34	29	29	32
Special Education	77	80	74	73	76	80
Bilingual Education	23	27	21	24	24	14
Assistance to Indochinese Refugee Children	8	11	8	2	3	0
Desegregation	8	11	6	6	3	6
Title IV—ESAA (Instructional)	64	61	65	68	68	62
Title III or IV C (Innovative Programs)	23	27	18	23	29	23
Other	6	5	6	9	6	1

mentioned them. Funded programs were found in 98 percent of the public schools, 89 percent of parochial schools, and none of the private, religious affiliated schools. Apparently, wide targeting of these funds has been successfully realized.

Interscholastic Sports

Interscholastic sports continues to be an important part of the program of middle level schools. The data in Tables 126 and 127 show that even at the fifth grade level 60 percent of the schools offered an interscholastic sports program, increasing to more than 90 percent at the ninth grade level. At all grade levels, basketball was the most popular boys' and girls' sport, followed by track, and then football for boys and volleyball for girls. Interestingly, wrestling was more popular for boys than our national pasttime, baseball, and soccer fared better than swimming or gymnastics. Softball and gymnastics were popular for girls.

When analyzed by grade levels, the sports data show some interesting tendencies. The 6-7-8 organization had the highest percentage of schools with *no* interscholastic sports programs for seventh and eighth

TABLE 126
Interscholastic Sports for Boys

	Grades 7	Grades 8	Grades 9	Grades 7	Grades 8	Grades 6	Grades 7	Grades 8	Grades 5	Grades 6	Grades 7	Grades 8
No inter. sports	12	10	7	12	10	32	18	16	40	31	6	9
Have inter. sports	88	90	93	88	90	68	82	84	60	69	94	91
Football	41	62	76	46	56	9	42	51	6	6	40	54
Basketball	66	80	85	76	81	26	72	80	20	29	77	86
Baseball	23	27	43	17	17	6	15	18	9	9	26	29
Softball	6	6	9	9	10	7	8	9	3	9	9	9
Track	67	74	82	67	70	19	53	58	11	14	66	66
Wrestling	46	51	54	36	38	8	24	27	0	3	34	37
Swimming	12	12	25	8	9	2	6	6	3	3	3	3
Gymnastics	12	13	19	10	11	4	4	5	3	3	3	3
Tennis	20	22	38	11	12	4	11	14	0	0	3	3
Volleyball	6	9	11	7	9	4	8	8	6	6	6	6
Soccer	15	15	20	21	21	12	16	18	3	9	17	6
Ice hockey	3	2	5	1	1	2	0	0	0	0	0	0

TABLE 127
Interscholastic Sports for Girls

	Grades 7	Grades 8	Grades 9	Grades 7	Grades 8	Grades 6	Grades 7	Grades 8	Grades 5	Grades 6	Grades 7	Grades 8
No inter. sports	12	10	6	12	11	32	18	16	40	34	9	9
Have inter. sports	88	90	94	88	89	68	82	84	60	66	91	91
Football	2	3	3	2	2	3	3	3	0	0	0	0
Basketball	63	74	79	69	76	23	67	72	17	26	60	69
Baseball	2	3	3	0	1	3	2	3	6	6	6	6
Softball	25	32	41	29	31	11	21	23	6	11	26	26
Track	66	72	79	65	69	19	55	57	9	14	66	60
Wrestling	2	3	4	2	2	1	0	0	0	0	0	0
Swimming	13	13	24	8	10	2	6	6	3	3	3	3
Gymnastics	24	27	36	18	19	4	9	10	3	3	6	6
Tennis	21	23	39	12	13	5	12	14	0	0	3	3
Volleyball	45	53	63	49	51	8	33	35	9	9	37	43
Soccer	9	10	10	15	16	9	13	13	3	6	11	11
Ice hockey	0	0	0	0	0	1	0	0	0	0	0	0

graders. Conversely, the 5-6-7-8 schools provided the most sports opportunities for them (90+ percent).

In most cases population was a minor factor in the availability of interscholastic sports. The schools in the more populated areas (150,000 or more) reported lower than typical percentages of football, track, basketball, wrestling, and volleyball. Small towns (5,000-24,999) showed the highest percentage of schools with interscholastic sports, at 96-97 percent.

Eighty-six percent of the principals who responded to the 1966 NASSP study indicated that they had some interscholastic athletics in their schools. The present data are comparable, suggesting considerable stability in these programs at the middle level.

Student Activities

Providing socialization activities for the developing pre and early adolescent remains a prominent responsibility of the middle level school. Table 128 details the types of extra/cocurricular activities available to grade 5-9 students. For the most part, 7-8-9 and 7-8 schools offered more activities than the other grade level configurations, except for intramurals where 6-7-8 schools showed higher percentages.

When student activities were compared by size of school, very few differences were found.

Articulation

Junior high and middle schools, because of their place in the "middle" of the educational structure, are faced with a task of coordination with both elementary and senior high schools. Principals were asked to indicate what problems existed in six areas of this articulation.

TABLE 128
Extra/Cocurricular Activities by Grade Level Organization

	Grades 7 8 9	Grades 7 8	Grades 6 7 8	Grades 5 6 7 8
Intramurals	68 67 63	70 69	80 79 79	57 66 66 63
Student government	91 91 90	84 84	77 80 82	46 51 77 77
Student clubs	81 81 82	66 67	55 59 59	29 34 43 46
Honor societies	32 46 50	34 36	18 30 31	3 3 17 17
Dramatics	50 59 67	50 54	31 43 47	11 14 34 40
Publications	51 62 81	63 73	46 54 64	14 20 34 46
Musical groups	90 92 92	89 89	86 91 90	60 63 69 69
Other	6 8 9	7 7	4 5 5	9 9 9 11

Information reported in Table 129 indicates that the major articulation problem with both elementary and secondary schools was coordination of the subject/content sequence. Almost half of the administrators expressed subject/content sequence problems. Schools with grades 5-6-7-8 reported the highest difficulty in this area—59 percent—with secondary schools. Schools with grades 7-8 had the greatest content articulation problem with elementary schools. Marking/grading and promotion policies also presented difficulty for 7-8 schools, with the elementary level.

Accreditation

Forty-eight percent of all middle level schools reported that they were accredited by a regional agency. Fifty-four percent of the 7-8-9 schools so indicated, probably reflecting the existing practices in accreditation toward the higher grade levels.

TABLE 129
Articulation Problems by Grade Level Organization

	Total	7-8-9	7-8	6-7-8	5-6-7-8	Other
With Elementary Level						
Student records	25	24	23	23	26	39
Pupil promotion policies	33	31	39	27	14	39
Granting of subject credit	11	8	10	14	17	15
Subject content/Sequence	48	48	52	44	44	42
Counseling services	37	38	35	36	32	39
Marking/Grading systems	34	31	40	34	29	25
With Secondary Level						
Student records	22	21	18	29	25	37
Pupil promotion policies	35	37	33	38	28	42
Granting of subject credit	24	27	19	24	29	24
Subject content/Sequence	49	47	50	52	59	27
Counseling services	30	24	32	39	44	25
Marking/Grading systems	22	18	26	30	35	15

TABLE 130
Regional Accreditation by Grade Level Organization

	Total	7-8-9	7-8	6-7-8	5-6-7-8	Other
Yes	48	54	45	35	40	59
No	52	46	55	65	60	41

TABLE 131
Parent Conferences

	Does your school have regularly scheduled parent conferences?					
	Total	7-8-9	7-8	6-7-8	5-6-7-8	Other
No	45	50	43	41	26	43
Yes (1-2/year)	46	41	49	49	53	45
Yes (3+/year)	9	9	8	10	21	12

Parent Conferences

Regularly scheduled parent conferences were reported by 55 percent of the schools (Table 131). Almost three-fourth of the 5-6-7-8 schools held one or more conferences annually. Generally speaking, regularly scheduled conferences were more likely to occur in middle schools and less so in junior high schools.

Use of Data Processing

When asked, "Does your middle level school use data processing machines?" 42 percent of the principals answered in the negative (Table 132). Indeed, there were marked differences in the degree of use when comparisons were made by grade level organization. Ninety-five percent of 5-6-7-8 schools reported no use of this technology while almost 75 percent of the 7-8-9 schools did so. Among schools employing data processing, scheduling use was reported by 50 percent, grade reporting by 46 percent, and record keeping by 38 percent. Schools with 7-8-9 grades again were the predominant users.

Per-pupil expenditure was a factor in the use of data processing. In all cases, the higher the pupil expenditure, the more the use of data processing. Curiously, schools with enrollments of 800-999 indicated the highest percentage of use.

TABLE 132
Data Processing by Grade Level

	Total	7-8-9	7-8	6-7-8	5-6-7-8	Other
No, do not have access to data processing machines	42	27	47	54	95	49
Yes, use them for scheduling	50	64	44	36	5	44
Yes, use them for record keeping	38	50	34	32	5	18
Yes, use them for grade reporting	46	61	40	29	5	38

Summary

School Organization

Ninety-eight percent of the schools surveyed were public. Parochial/diocesan and private, religious affiliated schools represented 1 percent of the sample respectively.

The most common grade level organization reported in this study was the 7-8-9 pattern (42 percent), followed by 7-8 (31 percent), 6-7-8 (15 percent), and 5-6-7-8 (4 percent). The highest percentage of change in grade levels during the last 10 years was reported by 6-7-8 schools. The most frequently mentioned reasons for change were to provide programs better suited to the middle level child and to provide a better transition from elementary to high school. These reasons represented a major change from Alexander's 1967 study where administrators most often cited "adjustment to enrollment trends."

Almost one-fifth (19 percent) of middle level schools reported per-pupil expenditures of $1,800 or more per year. Forty-three percent of the schools spent $1,200-1,799 and 38 percent had expenditures of less than $1,200.

A majority of principals indicated that their schools had the following facilities: gymnasiums, libraries, instructional materials centers, media centers, industrial arts labs, reading labs, music rooms, and art rooms.

Instructional Program

Principals indicated that students spend at least three-fourths of their instructional time in the traditional class size of 15-35 students. There was very little difference in the time spent in traditional classroom settings when students at the various grade level combinations were compared.

With the exception of the fifth grade, middle level students spend at least three-fourths of their time in the subject specialist format (one subject taught by one teacher). The higher the grade level, the higher the percentage of time spent in subject specialist classrooms. The lower the grade level, the more time spent in self-contained classrooms. Team teaching was most commonly found in sixth grade classrooms.

The five subjects of English/language arts, math, science, social studies, and physical education were almost universally required of all students at all grade levels. Instrumental music was the most popular elective course. The two most frequently mentioned supplementary programs (over and above the regular school program) were summer school and enrollment in high school courses.

Ability grouping was used in 88 percent of the schools. The three most frequently identified placement criteria were staff judgments, standardized tests, and grades. When principals were asked to indicate the scope of grouping policies in their schools, two-thirds of them reported using "grouping at all grade levels in certain subjects."

Seventy percent of the schools had programs for the gifted, the majority employing teacher recommendation and standardized tests for purposes of identification. These programs were most frequently offered in the "regular class with individual projects."

The three most frequently cited funded programs were Special Education, ESAA Title IV—Instructional, and ESEA Title I—Compensatory.

Sports were available to a majority of boys and girls at all grades in all grade level organizations. Basketball and track were identified as the most popular sports followed by football for boys and volleyball for girls. The most frequently identified student activities in middle level schools were musical groups, student government, clubs, and intramurals. For the most part, 7-8-9 schools more frequently reported a higher percentage of these activities.

The major articulation problem identified by middle level administrators was coordination of the subject/content sequence with elementary and secondary schools.

Forty-eight percent of the schools were accredited. Schools with grades 7-8-9 were much more likely to be accredited than 5-6-7-8 schools.

Over half of all schools held regularly scheduled parent conferences. Conferences were held most frequently in 5-6-7-8 schools.

A majority of principals from 7-8-9 schools reported regular use of data processing for scheduling, record keeping, and grade reporting.

V Principals View Middle Level Issues

More than 70 years have elapsed since the establishment of the first junior high school. During that time, many issues have been raised concerning appropriate programs and grade level organizations for the pre and early adolescent. This discussion has taken on new vigor in the past 20 years with the emergence of the "middle school."

The perceptions of middle level administrators regarding school purposes, programs, structures, and personnel issues are reported in this chapter.

TASKS OF AMERICAN SCHOOLS

Middle level principals were asked to rank statements about the educational purposes of American schools. The list of 11 statements developed for the 1978 NASSP study of the *Senior High School Principalship* was used so that comparison could be made with the perceptions of high school principals. Where parallel statements existed, comparisons were also made with the 1966 NASSP *Report of the Junior High-School Principalship*. Table 133 outlines these relationships.

Acquisition of basic skills was ranked number one in all three studies. Strong programs in essential learning areas continue to be a strong priority. There was also much agreement among middle and high school principals in the 1977 and 1980 studies on the ranking of the other tasks of education. Both groups agreed on the ranking of positive self-concept (#2), inquiry and problem solving skills (#3), moral and spiritual values (#4), physical fitness (#9), skills for a technological society (#10), and appreciation of the fine arts (#11).

Differences, although not major, appeared in the ranking of four areas: understanding of the American value system, career planning and training, preparation for a changing world, and preparation for family living.

Generally, middle level and high school principals are in fairly close agreement about the tasks of American schools.

A major difference appeared in the rankings of this 1980 study compared with the 1966 junior high study. "Development of positive self-concept and good human relations" was ranked sixth out of 9 in the 1966 study. Respondents in 1980 ranked it second out of 11 items, suggesting that current principals placed increased emphasis on the

TABLE 133
Task of American Schools

Rank NASSP 1980 Middle Level Study	Educational Task	NASSP 1966 Jr. High Study*	NASSP 1978 High School Study
1	Acquisition of basic skills (reading, writing, speaking, computing, etc.).	1	1
2	Development of positive self-concept and good human relations.	6	2
3	Development of skills and practice of critical intellectual inquiry and problem solving.	4.5	3
4	Development of moral and spiritual values.	2	4
5	Understanding of the American value system (its political, economic, social values, etc.).	4.5	7
6	Career planning and training in beginning occupational skills.	—	5
7	Preparation for a changing world.	7	8
8	Knowledge about and skills in preparation for family life (e.g., sex education, home management, problems of aging, etc.).	—	6
9	Physical fitness and useful leisure time sports.	8	9
10	Development of skills to operate in a technological society (engineering, scientific, etc.).	9	10
11	Appreciation for and experience with the fine arts.	—	11

*The third priority task in the 1966 Junior High Study, "Acquisition of basic knowledge" was not listed as a response alternative in either the current middle level study or the 1978 high school study.

importance of personal development. This same shift was evident at the senior high level. Principals ranked self-concept seventh out of 9 in the 1965 study and second out of 11 in the 1978 study.

MIDDLE LEVEL PROGRAMS

Opinions About Ability Grouping Policies

When asked, "What do you think should be done about ability grouping policy for a middle level school?" almost 60 percent of the principals selected ability grouping in all grade levels, but restricted to certain subject areas (Table 134). Only 8 percent said they favored no form of ability grouping. Five percent wrote in grouping practices other than those listed, singling out the following for preference:

- Grouping for high achievement, advanced placement, or the gifted;
- Special education and remedial programs;
- Flexible grouping within classroom based on need, achievement, and learning style.

Data presented in the previous chapter described current ability grouping practices in middle level schools. Information in Table 116 showed that 12 percent of the principals had no ability grouping in their schools, similar to the 8 percent above who had no preference for ability grouping. There was also consistency in practice and opinion about the types of grouping formats employed. Fifty-nine percent of the administrators both indicated the existence of and their personal preference for "grouping in all grades and in certain subjects." Degree of practice and preference were comparable for the other grouping formats.

Data by enrollment revealed an increasing preference for grouping in all grades and in certain subjects as schools increased in size.

In comparison with the 1966 Junior High School Study, very few differences were found either in grouping practices or in principal opinions about them. Table 135, however, does evidence a few trends. Grouping in all grades and all subjects declined in practice from 15 percent in 1966 to 9 percent in 1980. The percentage of principals who favored this form of ability grouping also declined from 19 percent in 1966 to 10 percent in 1980. The percentage of schools grouping students in all grades and in certain subjects increased by 6 percent (53 to 59 percent), paralleled by an increase in the percentage of principals who favored this grouping practice (52 to 59 percent). It is apparent that research on the largely unfavorable effects of ability grouping has yet to influence the level of practice.

TABLE 134
Opinions About Ability Grouping Policies by Grade Level Organization

	Total	7-8-9	7-8	6-7-8	5-6-7-8	Other
Grouping in all grades and in all subjects	10	10	9	12	15	27
Grouping in all grades and in certain subjects	59	56	64	56	45	53
Grouping in certain subjects and in all grade levels	1	2	2	1	5	0
Grouping in certain subjects and in certain grade levels	17	20	12	15	35	13
Should be a system different from alternatives listed	5	6	4	5	0	1
Should be no ability grouping	8	6	9	11	0	6

TABLE 135
Comparisons of NASSP 1980 and NASSP 1966 Studies on Current Ability Grouping Policy and Principal Opinion About Grouping Policies

	Current Policy Toward Ability Grouping		Opinion About Ability Grouping Policy	
	1980	1966	1980	1966
Grouping in all grades and in all subjects	9	15	10	19
Grouping in all grades and in certain subjects	59	53	59	52
Grouping in certain grades and in all subjects	2	5	1	3
Grouping in certain grades and in certain subjects	15	15	17	14
A system different from alternatives listed	4	3	5	4
No ability grouping	11	9	8	7

Opinions About Special Education

Most principals (68 percent) viewed special education as an integral part of the entire school program, suggesting that there is strong support among administrators for the "mainstreaming" concept. Thirty-one percent considered special education an important but supplemental program for selected students. Only 1 percent saw it as unnecessary or inappropriate.

Opinions About Individualized Promotion

Many educators feel that middle level schools should provide more individualized programs that would allow students to progress at individual rates and be eligible for promotion at various times during the school year. Administrators were asked: "Would you be in favor of some system of individualized promotion for students rather than the customary use of grade placement and year-end promotion?"

Table 136 reveals that the majority of principals from all grade level organizations favored individualized promotion, but less than 10 percent had such a system. The most striking contrast was in 5-6-7-8 schools where 70 percent of the administrators favored such a system but only 5 percent indicated that one was in operation.

When the data were examined by school size (Table 137), a majority of schools with enrollments below 1,400 favored an individualized promotion system. Principals of the largest schools (1,400 or more) were somewhat more opposed than favorable to the concept. This group of principals, however, reported the highest percentage of individualized promotion systems actually in operation (13 percent).

TABLE 136
Opinions About Individualized Promotion by Grade Level Organization

	Total	7-8-9	7-8	6-7-8	5-6-7-8	Other
Yes	56	56	59	53	70	50
Yes, and we have such a system	9	8	10	8	5	14
No	35	36	31	39	25	36

TABLE 137
Opinions About Individualized Promotion by Enrollment

	<400	400-599	600-799	800-999	1,000-1,399	1,400+
Yes	54	57	55	59	63	36
Yes, and we have such a system	7	8	12	10	7	13
No	39	35	33	31	30	51

Opinions About Competency Testing for Promotion

A majority of principals (54 percent) were quite ambivalent about the use of competency testing in basic skills for promotion (Table 138). Principals at the 6-7-8 grade schools had the strongest feelings about competency testing; about one-fourth expressed approval and one-fourth rejected the idea.

Enrollment appeared to be an important factor in the use of competency testing for promotion. Thirty-eight percent of the principals in

TABLE 138
Opinions About Competency Testing for Promotion by Grade Level

	Total	7-8-9	7-8	6-7-8	5-6-7-8	Other
Yes	17	15	19	23	11	14
Yes, and we have such a system	10	11	10	10	9	9
Some advantages/Some disadvantages	54	55	54	41	63	63
No	19	19	17	26	17	14

TABLE 139
Opinions About Competency Testing for Promotion by Enrollment

	<400	400-599	600-799	800-999	1,000-1,399	1,400+
Yes	22	17	16	15	17	11
Yes, and we have such a system	9	7	6	18	11	38
Some advantages/Some disadvantages	50	54	57	53	55	46
No	19	22	21	14	17	5

schools of 1,400 students or more reported having such a system in their schools and another 11 percent indicated they were in favor of it.

Opinions About Interscholastic Sports

Whether interscholastic athletic programs should be offered to middle level students has been a major issue for more than two decades. As early as 1952, a joint committee of elementary principals, National Education Association (NEA) members, and American Association of Health, Physical Education, and Recreation (AAHPER) members concluded that the high level of competition fostered by interscholastic athletics made them highly undesirable for children below the ninth grade level. The committee cited both emotional and physical reasons for its disapproval. In the intervening years many other groups have spoken for or against the inclusion of sports in middle level schools. Much concern has been expressed about keeping athletic programs "in proper perspective." The recent disclosure that in several states eighth grade football players were repeating the eighth grade in order to gain weight, speed, and maturity has prodded middle level educators to carefully examine their own athletic programs in terms of emphasis, priorities, and relationship to the total educational program of the school.

To assess current opinion of middle level administrators about sports, principals were asked to indicate whether interscholastic sports should be available to boys and girls in grades 5 through 9.

Table 140 shows that, even at the fifth and sixth grade levels, more than half of the administrators supported interscholastic athletics. At grades 7, 8, and 9, the response was overwhelmingly in favor of these programs. Supportive principals favored swimming, track, gymnastics, and basketball for fifth and sixth graders. Basketball and track were picked most frequently for grades 7, 8, and 9 (Table 141).

Opinions About Intramural Programs

Twenty-five percent of the respondents said that intramural programs should be emphasized more than interscholastic programs at *all* middle level grade levels. A majority of the principals (56 percent) felt

TABLE 140
Opinions Whether Interscholastic Sports Should Be Provided at the Middle Level

	\multicolumn{5}{c}{Grades}
	5	6	7	8	9
Yes	58	58	76	84	95
No	42	42	24	16	5

TABLE 141
Opinions About What Interscholastic Sports Should Be Provided at Middle Level*

Grade 5	Grade 6	Grade 7	Grade 8	Grade 9
Swimming	Track	Track	Basketball	Basketball
Track	Basketball	Basketball	Track	Track
Gymnastics	Swimming	Volleyball (G)	Volleyball (G)	Football (B)
Basketball	Gymnastics	Softball (G)	Football (B)	Volleyball (G)
Soccer	Soccer	Gymnastics	Softball (G)	Softball (G)
		Swimming	Gymnastics	Tennis
		Soccer	Soccer	Wrestling (B)
		Football (B)	Wrestling (B)	Gymnastics
		Wrestling (B)	Swimming	Baseball (B)
				Swimming
				Soccer

*Answers in order of frequency: B = Boys, G = Girls. Responses for boys and girls were similar on nonspecified listings.

that intramurals should be stressed at grade 8 and below. For grades 5 and 6, all of the respondents favored intramurals.

Principals in the 1966 study also gave strong support to intramural programs. A majority (55 percent) felt that "a well conducted after-school recreation and intramural program would be beneficial and would lead to a desirable reduction, if not a replacement, for present interschool athletic programs." Support continues to be strong for intramural programs at the middle level, but does not appear to have reduced or eliminated interest in interscholastic sports.

ORGANIZATION OF MIDDLE LEVEL SCHOOLS

Considerable debate has occurred over the issue of "ideal grade level organization" and the "optimal size" of middle level schools. Administrators' opinions about these two issues along with perceptions about community support for curriculum change and the use of technology will be presented in this section.

Ideal Grade Level Organizational Structure

A majority of principals (54 percent) indicated that the ideal grade level organizational structure was grades 6-7-8 (Table 142). The current grade level organization of the administrator's school had little influence on this choice.

When analyzed by region, population, and enrollment the data clearly established the ascendancy of the 6-7-8 structure. A *majority* of principals from all population areas and all but one region favored it. All enrollment categories ranked it first.

TABLE 142
Opinions About the Ideal Grade Organizational Structure for a Middle Level School

Choices	Total	7-8-9	7-8	6-7-8	5-6-7-8	Other
7-8-9	17	26	11	8	9	12
7-8	18	13	32	11	10	12
6-7-8	54	51	51	72	38	44
5-6-7-8	6	5	3	5	33	10
Other	5	5	3	4	10	22

TABLE 143
Opinions About the Ideal Middle Level Grade Organizational Structure by Region

	New England	Middle Atlantic	South	Midwest	Southwest	Rocky Mountain	Far West
7-8-9	13	15	22	12	24	23	24
7-8	17	12	11	19	29	17	24
6-7-8	50	61	52	58	43	53	50
5-6-7-8	15	7	6	4	1	3	1
Other	5	5	9	7	3	4	1

TABLE 144
Comparison of 1980 and 1966 NASSP Studies: Ideal Grade Level Organizational Structure

	NASSP 1980	NASSP 1966
7-8-9	17	65
7-8	18	13
6-7-8	54	18

In the 1966 NASSP study principals were asked, "What do you feel would be the ideal grade organization for a junior high school?" The grade level choices given to administrators in that study included: 7-9, 7-8, 6-8, 7-10, 6-9, K-8, and "other." The categories of 7-10, 6-9, K-8, and "other" received a combined 4 percent of the total. The 1980 study asked administrators to select from the 7-8-9, 7-8, 6-7-8, 5-6-7-8, and "other" categories. The responses to the three overlapping categories in the two studies are shown in Table 144.

Some dramatic changes have occurred since the 1966 study when 65 percent of the administrators selected the 7-8-9 school as the ideal grade level organization. In 1966, only 18 percent chose the 6-7-8 organization and 13 percent, the 7-8 structure. In the current study, opinion shifted overwhelmingly toward the 6-7-8 grouping (54 percent

FIGURE M (Based on Table 144)
Ideal Grade Level Structure: 1980 and 1966

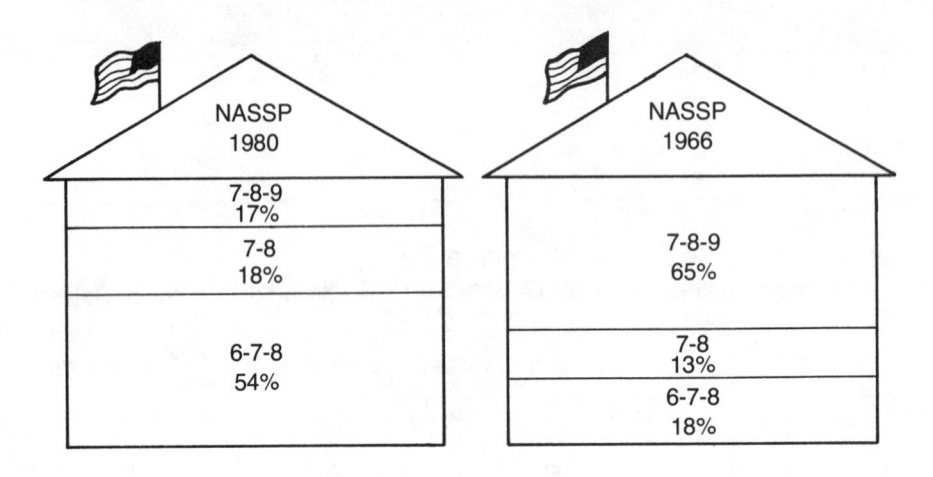

NASSP 1980:
- 7-8-9: 17%
- 7-8: 18%
- 6-7-8: 54%

NASSP 1966:
- 7-8-9: 65%
- 7-8: 13%
- 6-7-8: 18%

Source: Table 144

as opposed to 17 percent for 7-8-9). The 7-8 structure also registered a moderate increase in support. These changes are probably due in part to the fact that the middle school movement has gained momentum in the past 20 years.

Optimum Middle Level School Size

Schools of 600-799 students were seen by 36 percent of the respondents as the optimum size (Table 145). Forty-four percent of the 7-8-9 principals indicated a preference for a school with 600-799 students. Forty-five percent of those in 5-6-7-8 schools preferred enrollments of 400-599. Sixty percent of the 6-7-8 principals opted for schools in the enrollment range of 400-799. Generally speaking, principals of schools with the upper middle level grades favored larger enrollments while those with lower middle level grades favored smaller ones.

TABLE 145
Opinions About Optimal Number of Students for a Middle Level School by Grade Level Organization

	Total	7-8-9	7-8	6-7-8	5-6-7-8	Other
<400	12	6	17	10	30	14
400-599	27	21	33	30	45	23
600-799	36	44	32	30	20	40
800-999	17	20	13	18	5	14
1,000-1,399	8	8	5	12	0	9
1,400+	0	1	0	0	0	0

TABLE 146
Opinions About Optimal Number of Students for a Middle Level School by Enrollment

	<400	400-599	600-799	800-999	1,000-1,399	1,400+
<400	54	6	1	2	0	0
400-599	33	50	17	8	3	21
600-799	12	36	62	35	30	0
800-999	<1	7	15	43	39	26
1,000-1,399	<1	1	5	12	25	36
1,400+	0	0	0	0	3	17

Not surprisingly, the size of the principal's current school appeared to be a strong influencing factor in the selection of "optimal school size." For each of the first four choices, 399 or less, 400-599, 600-799, and 800-999, the highest percentage of administrators favoring that choice were incumbents at that enrollment range. Principals apparently are satisfied enough with the current size of their schools.

Opinions About Curricular Change and Community Support

When asked if public schools should obtain community support before making important curricular changes, two-thirds of the principals expressed agreement to strong agreement. Twenty-four percent disagreed while the remainder (10 percent) had ambivalent feelings.

Principals in the 1966 NASSP study were evenly divided on this issue with 49 percent reporting agreement and 51 percent, disagreement. During the past 14 years, principals have come to view more positively the involvement of the community in curriculum change.

Opinions About Technological Advances

Many educators and the lay public feel that technological advances such as television and computer-assisted instruction offer real promise for improving middle level education. Principals in this study agreed. Seventy percent saw technology holding some or considerable promise for improving the quality of their schools. Twenty-nine percent viewed it as not very helpful and 1 percent believed it would be harmful.

PERSONNEL ISSUES

The final section of this chapter examines principals' opinions about the characteristics and preparation of middle level teachers, why teachers change from middle level schools to other levels, and whether or not principals should have tenure.

Personal Characteristics of Teachers

Principals were asked to examine a list of 10 *personal* characteristics of middle level teachers and to assess the importance of each for teacher success. Table 147 lists the 10 characteristics. Ninety-seven percent of the administrators rated all 10 categories important or very important. The five statements identified as most important were:

- Ability to work with students and bring out their best capabilities.
- Ability to interact constructively with students and peers.
- Respect for the dignity and worth of the individual.
- Understanding the students' skills, abilities, and interests.
- Possess a positive self-concept.

Of the 10 characteristics, sensitivity to student cultural heritage and socioeconomic background was highly ranked least often. In view of contemporary concern with desegregation, multicultural issues, and compensatory education programs, one might have expected these characteristics to have been more highly considered.

TABLE 147
Personal Characteristics of Teachers and Their Importance to Successful Teaching

Characteristic	Not Important	Important	Very Important
Able to interact constructively with students and peers	1	6	93
Able to work with students and bring out students' best capabilities	0	6	94
Be a good model	0	26	74
Committed to education of early adolescents	1	24	75
Flexible	0	22	78
Positive self-concept	0	19	81
Respect the dignity and worth of the individual	0	10	90
Sensitive to cultural heritage of students	2	43	55
Sensitive to socioeconomic background of the students	3	46	51
Understand the students' skills, abilities, and interests	0	15	85

TABLE 148
Professional Characteristics of Teachers and Their Importance to Successful Teaching

The ability to:	Not Important	Important	Very Important
Counsel students	1	41	58
Promote independent learning among students	<1	40	60
Teach communication skills	<1	26	74
Use techniques of inquiry oriented problem solving	2	54	44
Utilize multimedia approaches to instruction	6	65	29
Use positive methods of classroom control	<1	13	87
Utilize values clarification activities appropriately	5	60	35
Employ varied learning strategies (not merely lecture and recitation)	1	14	85
Work across interdisciplinary lines	5	56	39
Work as a member of a teaching team	13	48	39

Professional Characteristics of Teachers

Principals were also asked to evaluate a listing of 10 *professional* characteristics of teachers as they related to successful middle level teaching. These characteristics are outlined in Table 148. With the exception of "Work as a member of teaching team," all characteristics were rated important to very important by at least 90 percent of the respondents. Positive methods of classroom control and use of varied learning strategies far outranked other alternatives. Teaching communication skills, promoting independent learning, and counseling students were also highly rated. Multimedia expertise in designing instruction was relatively less important than other characteristics in the view of most respondents.

Appropriate Professional Preparation of Teachers

In an attempt to survey perceptions of preservice education, the study looked at course work for the preparation of middle level teachers. The rankings of respondents are arranged in priority order in Table 149.

FIGURE N (Based on Table 149)
Ranking of Special Preservice Middle Level Courses

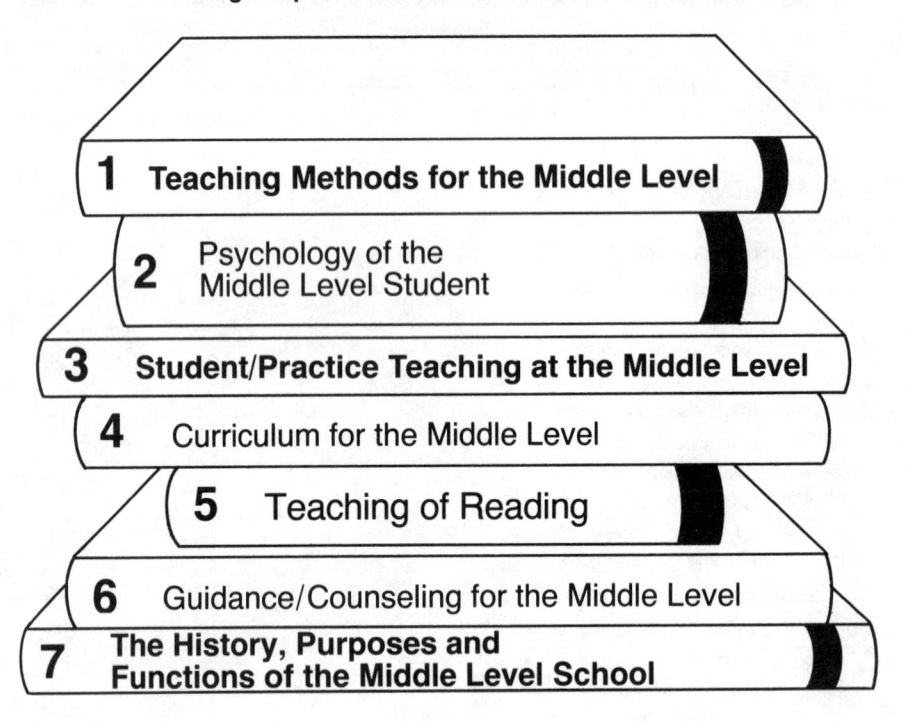

1. Teaching Methods for the Middle Level
2. Psychology of the Middle Level Student
3. Student/Practice Teaching at the Middle Level
4. Curriculum for the Middle Level
5. Teaching of Reading
6. Guidance/Counseling for the Middle Level
7. The History, Purposes and Functions of the Middle Level School

TABLE 149
Ranking of Special Preservice Middle Level Courses

(1) Teaching methods for the middle level.
(2) Psychology of the middle level student.
(3) Student/Practice teaching at the middle level.
(4) Curriculum for the middle level.
(5) Teaching of reading.
(6) Guidance/Counseling for the middle level.
(7) The history, purposes, and functions of the middle level school.

Table 150 presents a comparison of these preservice course rankings with those of the NASSP 1966 study. The two NASSP studies had comparable items both in subject matter and number. Some minor changes in opinion are evident in the intervening years. Middle level teaching methods moved from third place in 1966 to first place in 1980. Educational psychology and student teaching made similar shifts. Both studies ranked these preservice practices as the most appropriate for middle level teachers. "The history, purposes, and functions of the middle level school" was the lowest ranked item.

TABLE 150

Ranking of Special Preservice Middle Level Courses—NASSP 1980 and NASSP 1966

	NASSP 1980	NASSP 1966
Teaching methods for middle level	1	3
Psychology of the middle level student	2	1
Student/Practice teaching at the middle level	3	2
Curriculum for the middle level	4	6
Teaching of reading	5	4
Guidance/Counseling for the middle level	6	5
History, purposes, and functions of the middle level school	7	7

With the increased emphasis on skills, it is perplexing that reading was not ranked higher. In fact, when compared to the 1966 NASSP study, reading dropped a notch. Perhaps the implication here is that reading is more and more viewed as a specific core subject matter domain than a general area of teacher preparation.

Teacher Mobility

When asked to rank eight reasons why middle level teachers left to teach at either high schools or elementary schools, principals singled out teacher desire to work with different aged students as the most prominent. The eight reasons, in rank order, were:

1. Desire to work with different aged students.
2. Subject matter interests better met at other level.
3. Lack of adequate preparation to teach at the middle level.
4. Lack of status and/or recognition at the middle level.
5. Pupil-teacher ratio better at other level.
6. Better facilities.
7. More preparation time.
8. More money.

It is certainly understandable that some teachers leave middle level schools because they prefer to work with students of a different age. It is widely recognized that early adolescence is a difficult time in a person's life and that youngsters of this age present a special challenge to their teachers. Some teachers may not have the skill, patience, or personality to deal with this age group. Others may simply desire a change of pace as their interests shift from those of young adulthood to middle age, to approaching retirement.

The other reasons listed for mobility are symptomatic of the problems affecting middle level education. Some teachers placed at the middle level may feel their subject matter interests can better be met at other levels. Others may be victims of inadequate preparation to teach at the middle level. Teacher education programs prepare teachers to teach in elementary or high schools with little or no concern for the special problems and issues facing middle level schools. Those who prepare for teaching in secondary education departments face heavy demands for subject area competence. These teachers particularly may feel frustrated when they find that middle level students are not ready emotionally or intellectually to handle heavy doses of specialized subject matter.

Indeed, "lack of status and/or recognition at the middle level" represents a major problem for middle level educators. For many years the importance of middle level schools was underestimated. Most teachers were not prepared to teach "in the middle" and many simply waited for an opportunity to move to a high school position. Until recently most did not see working at a middle level school as a career goal. Fortunately, more appropriate teacher education programs are being established, better research is being conducted on early adolescence, and concerted effort is underway toward the improvement of middle level instructional programs.

Principal Tenure

Most principals do not appear to be tenured. Only 35 percent of the study respondents answered affirmatively to the fact of their personal tenure. When these same administrators were asked if they felt principals should have tenure, 64 percent replied in the affirmative.

Population and enrollment were important variables in administrator opinion regarding tenure. Almost 20 percent more of the principals in the largest population areas (150,000+) favored tenure than their counterparts elsewhere. Generally speaking, the larger the school the higher the percentage of principals in favor of tenure. (An exception to this trend was found in schools with enrollment of more than 1,400 students.)

Regional information (Table 151) showed that administrators in the Middle Atlantic region had the highest percentage of support for tenure (88 percent). A majority of administrators (55 percent) from the Far West were opposed.

TABLE 151
Opinions Regarding Support for Administrative Tenure by Region

	Total	New England	Middle Atlantic	South	Midwest	Southwest	Rocky Mountain	Far West
Yes	64	70	88	76	55	70	53	45
No	36	30	12	24	45	30	47	55

Summary

TASKS OF AMERICAN SCHOOLS

Principals indicated that the most important tasks of American schools were helping students acquire basic skills, positive self-concepts, and critical inquiry/problem solving skills. High school principals surveyed in the 1978 NASSP High School Study assigned top priority to these same purposes.

MIDDLE LEVEL PROGRAMS

Ability grouping was approved by more than 92 percent of middle level administrators and some form of ability grouping was present in 89 percent of their schools. The most favored form of ability grouping was grouping in all grades and in certain subjects.

Two-thirds of the principals viewed special education as an integral part of the school program.

A majority of principals (56 percent) favored individualized promotion programs, but only 9 percent reported one in operation at their schools.

Administrators have many reservations about competency testing for promotion. Fifty-four percent of the principals saw both advantages and disadvantages of the practice. Ten percent had existing programs in their schools, 17 percent were supportive, and 19 percent were opposed.

Sports programs were favored for both boys and girls at all grade levels by a majority of principals. Swimming, track, and basketball were the most frequently suggested sports for fifth and sixth graders. The most often cited sports for seventh, eighth, and ninth graders were basketball and track.

A majority of the administrators felt that intramurals should be emphasized over interscholastics in grade 8 and below. At grades 5 and 6, all respondents favored emphasis on intramurals.

ORGANIZATION OF MIDDLE LEVEL SCHOOLS

Principals generally supported a 6-7-8 grade organizational structure for middle level schools. When these findings were compared with the NASSP 1966 study, it was evident that a major shift in opinion had occurred. The ideal grade level structure in the earlier study, the 7-8-9 school, dropped from 65 percent in 1966 to 17 percent in the current study. The 6-7-8 grade format rose from 18 percent in 1966 to 54 percent in 1980.

No particular school size was highly regarded over others. The largest percentage of principals (36 percent) favored schools with enrollments of 600-799. In most cases respondents indicated that the optimum school size was the same as the school in which they were presently serving as principals.

Two-thirds of the administrators agreed that schools should not make important curricular changes without first securing community support. Almost one-fourth, however, felt that it was not necessary to seek community support prior to change.

In the opinion of 70 percent of the principals, technological advances such as television and computer-assisted instruction held some promise for improving the quality of instruction in middle level schools.

PERSONNEL ISSUES

The top-ranked *personal* characteristics for middle level teaching were: ability to work with students and bring out the students' best capabilities; ability to interact constructively with students and peers; respect for the dignity and worth of the individual; an understanding of the students' skills, abilities, and interests; and possession of a positive self-concept.

Principals ranked positive methods of classroom control, use of varied learning strategies, and the ability to teach communication skills as the most important middle level teacher *professional* characteristics.

Among seven forced-choice alternatives, respondents named teaching methods for the middle level, psychology of the middle level student, and student/practice teaching at a middle level school as the most appropriate experiences for the preparation of middle level teachers.

Desire to work with different-aged students, subject matter interests better met at the other levels, and lack of adequate preparation to teach at the middle school level were identified as major reasons why teachers move to high schools or elementary schools.

Principals favored administrative tenure by a two-to-one majority. Administrators from large population areas, large schools, and the Middle Atlantic region supported tenure by much higher percentages than did other administrators. A majority of principals from the Far West (55 percent) were opposed to administrative tenure.

VI Principal and Program Profiles

The issues of middle level education have been reported, analyzed, and discussed in the earlier chapters of this report. What emerges is a picture of middle level schooling that confirms many of the expectations of avid middle level watchers. That picture is generally a comely portrait distinguished by a firm commitment to student developmental needs.

It is important to remember that we have described the middle level school as operationally encompassing any grade or grade combinations from grade 5 through 9. This definition embraces both traditional junior high school organizations and the more recent "middle school" patterns. Schools with grades above or below these parameters have been deliberately excluded from study consideration. Our conclusions reflect this focus as well as the limitations of our sample.

A number of questions were raised in the Introduction and Chapter I that bear on the fundamental *raison d'etre* of middle-level schooling. This chapter summarizes the answers to these questions, which probe the status and direction of education at this level as perceived by its principals:

1. What are the characteristics of the 1980 middle level principal?

2. What are the demographic characteristics of middle level schools?

3. What are the programs currently employed in middle level education throughout the United States?

4. How do principals view the most significant program and personnel issues of the middle level?

5. How do present middle school principals differ from junior high school principals?

6. Are middle schools significantly different from junior high schools in staffing and enrollment, instructional system, and program organization?

7. Has the middle school established itself as a unique level of education?

1. THE PRINCIPAL

The 1980 middle level principals are older, more experienced, and better educated than their counterparts in the 1966 NASSP study.

Personal Characteristics

A. The typical principal is:
   - A white male;
   - Aged 45 to 54;
   - Possessor of a master's degree in secondary school administration plus additional graduate credits;
   - A former social studies teacher;
   - A former assistant principal.
B. There is a greater likelihood than in 1966 that the middle level principal will be female. The data show a higher percentage of female principals in:
   - Schools that do not include the ninth grade;
   - Cities of 150,000 population or greater;
   - Districts where the per-pupil expenditure is $1,200 or less;
   - The Far West region.
C. Generally middle level principals are older in schools that:
   - Include the ninth grade;
   - Are found in large cities;
   - Have 1,000 or more pupils.
D. Only 8 percent of the study respondents identified themselves as "other than white." A higher than average percentage of nonwhites is found among the following:
   - Female participants;
   - Large cities;
   - Schools where the per-pupil expenditure is $1,200 or less;
   - The South and Far West.

Professional Characteristics

E. The survey data on age at the time of the first principalship indicate that:
   - Beginning principals are typically appointed between the ages of 30 and 39;
   - Males attain their first principalship at an earlier age than females;
   - Principals beginning in junior high schools (grades 7-8-9) are older;
   - Principals who start in rural areas and small towns are younger;
   - Principals beginning in smaller schools are younger.

F. The turnover rate among middle level principals is no greater than at the time of the 1966 study. Respondents in a few categories had fewer years in their present principalship than the total sample:
- Females;
- Principals in junior high schools (grades 7-8-9);
- Those in the Far West.

G. Virtually all principals hold a master's degree or higher. More females than males earn the doctorate. Most principals revealed:
- Their undergraduate degree was from a public college or university;
- Their undergraduate major was not professional education;
- They had pursued graduate work beyond the master's degree.

H. The majority of the middle level principals:
- Have secondary school principal licenses;
- Earn salaries between $20,000 and $35,000 on their own (not teacher) schedules;
- Have 10½ month contracts or longer.

I. More principals participated in professional activities and fewer in community activities than those of the 1966 NASSP study. Most respondents like their work and would make the same career choice again. If they moved, it would be to a central office position.

Job Characteristics

J. The typical principal at the middle level feels that the job is self-fulfilling, prestigious, and secure. Most principals:
- Average more than 50 hours in their work week, females somewhat more than males;
- Spend the most time in school management functions;
- Would prefer to concentrate on program development activities;
- Have no classroom teaching responsibilities.

K. Principals in larger communities and districts have less authority over staff selection and budget control.

L. The major roadblocks to principal job performance are:
- Administrative detail;
- Apathetic or irresponsible parents;
- Problem students;
- Inability to obtain funding;
- Lack of time for self;
- Variations in the ability and dedication of staff members.

2. THE SCHOOLS

Schools at the middle level tend to mirror the communities they serve.

A. Middle level schools exhibit a recent noticeable increase in the size and diversity of staff:
   - Three-quarters have assistant principals and instructional aides.
   - Virtually all have librarians/media specialists, office secretaries/clerks, counselors, and special education teachers.
   - Women predominate on the teaching staff; men, on the administrative staff. Teacher preparation for middle level teaching has shown some progress.
B. Teacher-pupil ratios reflect school size and expenditure:
   - Schools with fewer than 800 students show typical ratios in the 1:21-25 range.
   - Larger schools average 1:26-30.
   - Many schools having more than 1,400 students show ratios of 1:31-35.
   - Schools spending more money have proportionately lower ratios.
C. Average daily attendance (ADA) reflects school size and grade organization.
   - Many schools with fewer than 800 students show ADA's in the 96+ range.
   - Nearly half of the schools with more than 1,400 students have ADA's at or below 90 percent.
   - Virtually all 5-6-7-8 grade schools indicate ADA's better than 90 percent.
   - Single grade schools evidence the lowest average ADA's.
D. Median school size is between 600 and 800 students. Junior highs tend to be larger; middle schools, smaller.
E. Small towns and rural areas report increasing parental desire for involvement.
F. Metropolitan areas are most affected by community pressure groups; suburban and rural areas are the least affected. Most of the pressure comes from other educational organizations (elementary and high schools, teacher associations, PTA/PTOs).

3. SCHOOL PROGRAMS

School and program organization evidence some change in the past decade.

School Organization

A. Schools in this study are more likely to be:
   - Public schools; nonpublic schools represent only 2 percent of the sample;
   - Grades 7-8-9 and 7-8 in organizational pattern;
   - Found in the Midwest region;
   - Located in the Rocky Mountain and Far West, if junior high schools;
   - Located in the Southwest and New England, if middle schools;
   - Larger if junior highs, smaller if middle schools.
B. Most frequently cited reasons for switching to a "middle school" grade level organization are:
   - Provide programs suited to middle level children;
   - Provide better transition from elementary to high school;
   - Adjust to enrollment trends.
C. A majority of principals report the following types of facilities in their schools:
   - Gymnasium
   - Library
   - Instructional materials center
   - Media center
   - Industrial arts lab
   - Reading lab
   - Music room
   - Art room

Program Organization

D. Instructional organization tends toward the traditional:
   - At least three-fourths of instructional time is spent in conventional classes of 15-35 students with one subject matter specialist.
   - English/language arts, math, science, social studies, and physical education are required courses.
   - Ability grouping is used at all grade levels in certain subjects with placement based on staff judgments, standardized tests, and student grades.
E. Most schools provide special programs in:
   - Summer school;
   - ESEA Title I, Compensatory;
   - ESAA Title IV, Instructional;
   - Special Education;

- Education of the gifted, with student selection based on standardized test scores and teacher recommendations and a process that emphasizes individual projects in regular classes.
F. Cocurricular programs most frequently offered are:
    - Boys interscholastic sports of basketball, track, and football;
    - Girls interscholastic sports of basketball, track, and volleyball;
    - Student activities in music, student government, clubs, and intramurals.
G. The major articulation problem for all middle level schools is coordination of the subject/content sequence with elementary and secondary schools.
H. About half of the schools reported these evaluation practices:
    - Accreditation by a regional agency;
    - Regular parental conferences;
    - Use of data processing for scheduling, record keeping, and grade reporting.

4. PRINCIPALS' VIEW OF ISSUES

Respondents' views of program and personnel issues reflect both a conventional and an emerging vision of middle level education.

Program

A. The most important tasks of American schools are helping students:
    - Acquire basic skills;
    - Develop positive self-concept and good human relations;
    - Develop critical inquiry and problem solving skills.
B. The majority of principals advocate:
    - Ability grouping in all grades and in certain subjects;
    - Special education as an integral part of the school program;
    - Individualized promotion;
    - Interscholastic sports for both boys and girls in all grade levels;
    - Emphasis on intramurals at grade 8 and below rather than on interscholastic sports.
C. Principals generally support:
    - A 6-7-8 grade organization as the ideal middle level pattern, regardless of the organizational structure of their own schools;
    - Their current school size as optimum;
    - The promise of technological advances to improve instructional quality.

Personnel

D. Principals cite these *personal* traits as the most significant for middle level teaching:
   - Ability to work with students and bring out their best capabilities;
   - Ability to interact constructively with students and peers;
   - Respect for the worth and dignity of the individual;
   - Understanding the students' skills, abilities, and interests;
   - Positive self-concept.
E. Principals ranked these *professional* characteristics of teachers as most important:
   - Use of positive methods of classroom control;
   - Use of varied learning strategies (not merely lecture and recitation);
   - Ability to teach communication skills.
F. The most appropriate experiences for the *preparation* of middle level teachers are:
   - Teaching methods for the middle level;
   - Psychology of the middle level student;
   - Student/practice teaching at the middle level.
G. Principals feel that teachers move to elementary or high school positions because they:
   - Desire to work with different-aged students;
   - Believe subject-matter interests are better met at the other level;
   - Lack adequate preparation to teach at the middle level.
H. Principals favor administrative tenure by a two-thirds majority.

5. PRINCIPAL DIFFERENCES

There are more similarities than differences among principals of middle level and junior high schools. Most of the dissimilarities fall in the personal/professional category and relate to professional preparation and status considerations. There are few task differences. The similarities are outlined in sections 1-4 of this chapter. The differential tendencies are summarized below (contrasting the 5-8 middle school pattern with the 7-9 junior high school).

Personal/Professional Characteristics

Middle School Principals	*Junior High School Principals*
▪ Somewhat younger in age	▪ Somewhat older
▪ Younger at first principalship	▪ Older at first principalship

- Fewer years in the principalship
- Fewer years in the position prior to the principalship
- Fewer years in current school
- A former assistant principal of a high school or principal of an elementary or high school
- An undergraduate major in elementary education or physical education
- No doctorate
- Administrative certification at the secondary or elementary level
- Annual salary below $25,000
- Nontenured
- More upwardly mobile

- More years in the principalship
- More years in the position prior to the principalship
- More years in current school
- A former assistant principal of a middle level or high school
- An undergraduate major in social science
- Holder of a doctorate
- Administrative certification at the secondary level
- Annual salary above $25,000
- Tenured
- Satisfied in the middle level principalship

Job Tasks

Middle School Principals

- Somewhat more authority in staffing and budget decisions
- Rate personal prestige and self-fulfillment at an above average level

Junior High School Principals

- Somewhat less authority in staffing and budget decisions
- Rate personal prestige and self-fulfillment at a moderate level

6. PROGRAM DIFFERENCES

Are there significant program differences between junior high schools and middle schools? How do the latter differ from the former in such structural elements as staffing and enrollment, instructional system, and program organization?

The differences reported below seem largely to reflect the different age ranges of the two organizational configurations. Middle schools with fifth and sixth graders are more structured and seem to assume a clear middle position between elementary and high school. Junior highs with ninth graders have more elaborate programs and facilities that emulate the traditional secondary patterns of organization.

Staffing and Enrollment

Middle Schools	Junior High Schools
■ Predominance of female teachers	■ Fewer female teachers
■ Somewhat higher teacher-pupil ratios	■ Somewhat lower teacher-pupil ratios
■ Located more often in rural areas	■ Located more often in cities and suburbs
■ Smaller enrollments	■ Larger enrollments
■ Better attendance records	■ Poorer attendance records
■ Greater parent/citizen involvement in school operational functions	■ Greater parent involvement in planning/advisory functions

School Programs

Middle Schools	Junior High Schools
■ Changed grade level pattern in past 10 years	■ Retained same grade level pattern for 16+ years
■ Less elaborate facilities	■ More comprehensive facilities
■ More required courses	■ More electives available
■ Fewer optional programs (e.g., summer school)	■ More optional programs
■ Somewhat less use of ability grouping	■ Somewhat greater use of ability grouping
■ Fewer programs for the gifted	■ More programs for the gifted
■ Interscholastic sports programs with 7-8 grade emphasis	■ Interscholastic sports programs for all grade levels
■ Fewer extra/cocurricular activities	■ More extra/cocurricular activities
■ Not regionally accredited	■ Regional accreditation
■ Greater incidence of regularly scheduled parent conferences	■ Fewer parent conferences
■ Less use of data processing	■ Greater use of data processing

7. A UNIQUE LEVEL

The middle level school has established itself as a unique level of education, catering to the developmental needs of the emerging adolescent. In this study, principals were asked to respond to several questions dealing explicitly with the rationale and organization of middle level schooling. Their responses are indicative of the emerging identity of this level of education.

A. Principals believe that a 6-7-8 organizational pattern is the most appropriate one for education at the middle level. They reported this preference (in Table 148) regardless of the grade level organizations of their own schools. Moreover, a majority of principals in all population areas, enrollment categories, and all but one region favor the 6-7-8 pattern.

Organizational Structure Alternatives (%)

	Total	Grades 7-8-9	Grades 7-8	Grades 6-7-8	Grades 5-6-7-8	Other Grades
7-8-9	17	26	11	8	9	12
7-8	18	13	32	11	10	12
6-7-8	(54)	(51)	(51)	(72)	(38)	(44)
5-6-7-8	6	5	3	5	33	10
Other	5	5	3	4	10	22

B. The study looked at course work for the preparation of middle level teachers. Principals' rank order of the most desirable course work clearly suggests the emergence of a definable middle level:
- Teaching methods for the middle level;
- Psychology of the middle level student;
- Student/practice teaching at the middle level;
- Curriculum for the middle level.

C. Reasons given by the 25 percent of the respondents who reported a change to a 5-6-7-8 or 6-7-8 organizational pattern reveal that educational rather than demographic considerations now more often motivate such changes (listed by rank order):
- Provide a program suited to the middle level child;
- Provide a better transition from elementary to high school;
- Adjust to enrollment trends.

6-7-8

ECONOMIC INFLUENCES

SOCIAL INFLUENCES

7-8-9

5-6-7-8

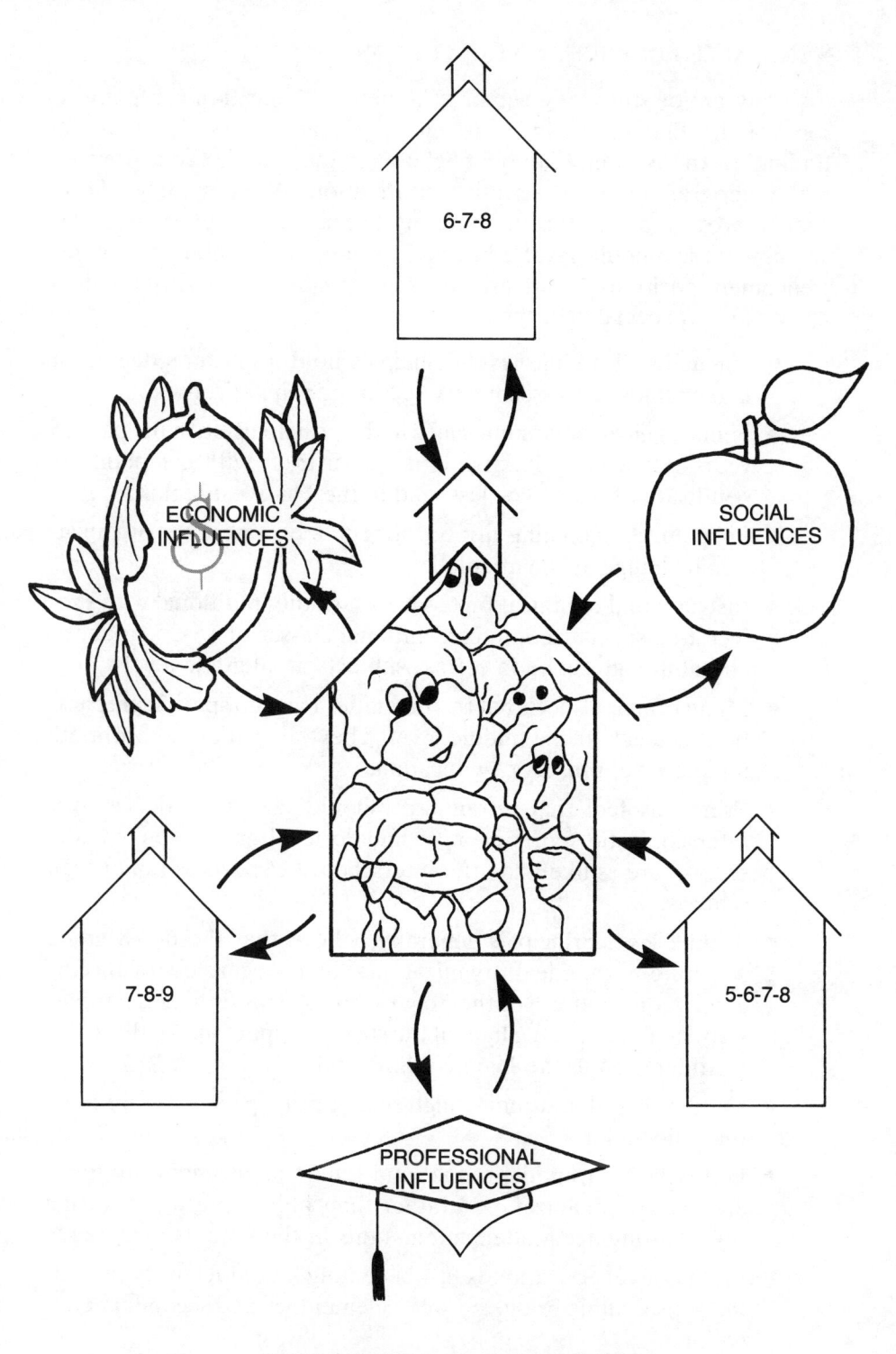

PROFESSIONAL INFLUENCES

SCHOOLS IN THE MIDDLE

8. Notable Findings and Conclusions

Any major study of a sector of American education can point to some of its findings as more noteworthy than others. Most of the findings of the National Study of Schools in the Middle are concerned with demographic and descriptive information. A few findings, however, are of greater interest, primarily because they reflect new developments in middle level education or support maintenance or retrenchment positions. There are no real surprises, but some of the data are worthy of special reflection.

- Virtually all middle level principals hold a master's degree or higher; most have secondary school principal licenses.
- Females have made some gains in the principalship in the past 15 years, particularly in large cities, in districts with per-pupil expenditure of $1,200 or less, and in the Far West region.
- Program is becoming a more acceptable reason for organizational change at the middle level.
- Instructional organization tends toward the traditional with subject area specialization, conventional classes of 15-35 students, and ability grouping in certain subjects at all grade levels.
- Many principals feel that their faculties have no specific preparation to teach at the middle level. They favor more appropriate middle level preservice education.
- Principals feel that intramurals should take precedence over interscholastic sports in most middle level grades, but middle schools are as likely to offer interscholastic sports as junior high schools.
- Middle level principals generally believe that the 6-7-8 grade structure is the ideal organizational plan, regardless of the organizational pattern of their own schools. This finding is particularly significant in the light of the strong support shown the 7-8-9 configuration in the 1966 NASSP study.
- Middle school and junior high school principals are more alike than dissimilar.
- Differences in middle school and junior high school programs are largely organizational rather than philosophical, reflecting the differing age/grade combinations in the schools.
- Middle level education is fast becoming a unique entity providing a discernible bridge between elementary and secondary education.

APPENDIX A

NATIONAL ASSOCIATION OF SECONDARY SCHOOL PRINCIPALS
Reston, Virginia 22091

A National Study of Schools in the Middle
Survey of Middle Level Principals (Form A)
Supported by the Geraldine R. Dodge Foundation

DIRECTIONS

Your questionnaire is identified by the label placed on it. It is not necessary to sign or place your name on the questionnaire. In reporting results, only statistical summaries of the responses of groups of principals will be cited. In no case will the identity of an individual be divulged. You are urged to make every answer a sincere one.

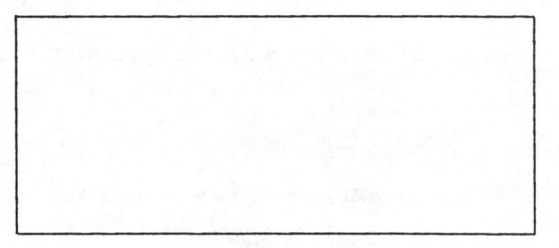

Circle the number of the appropriate response using pen or pencil. If you change a response, please make the change distinctly so there is no doubt about how you wish to answer.

Attempt to answer every question. For some questions none of the alternatives may correspond exactly to your situation or to the opinion you hold. In such cases mark the alternative which comes closest to the answer you would like to give.

For the purposes of this study, two terms should be clarified:

(1) *Middle level of education* is a general phrase used to encompass various combinations of grades five through nine.

(2) *Principal* refers to the chief building administrator and should not be confused with the role of assistant principal or vice principal, unless specifically stated.

Place your completed questionnaire in the envelope provided and mail it to NASSP. Thank you for your cooperation and assistance in this important study.

Steering Committee for the Study of Schools in the Middle:

Donald A. Stokes, King Junior High School, Portland, Maine; Kenneth M. Brashear, Comstock Middle School, Dallas, Tex.; Eugene B. Jump, Morgan Junior High School, Ellensburg, Wash.; Will Ella Brown, King Middle School, Dorchester, Mass.; Tom Maglaras, Aurora, Colo., Schools; Robert Mills, Central Michigan University.

Research Team:

Jerry Valentine, University of Missouri; Neal C. Nickerson, Jr., University of Minnesota; Anthony Gregorc, University of Connecticut; James W. Keefe, NASSP.

A2

1. What is your sex? (1) Male (2) Female

2. What is your age?
   - (1) 23 or under
   - (2) 24-29
   - (3) 30-34
   - (4) 35-39
   - (5) 40-44
   - (6) 45-49
   - (7) 50-54
   - (8) 55-59
   - (9) 60 or older

3. With what ethnic group would you identify yourself?
   - (1) White
   - (2) Black
   - (3) Chicano/Hispanic
   - (4) American Indian
   - (5) Asian
   - (6) Other: _____

4. At what age were you appointed to your first principalship?
   - (1) 23 or under
   - (2) 24-29
   - (3) 30-34
   - (4) 35-39
   - (5) 40-44
   - (6) 45-49
   - (7) 50-54
   - (8) 55-59
   - (9) 60 or older

5. How many years have you served as a principal, including this current year?
   - (1) One year
   - (2) 2 - 3 years
   - (3) 4 - 5 years
   - (4) 6 - 7 years
   - (5) 8 - 9 years
   - (6) 10 - 14 years
   - (7) 15 - 19 years
   - (8) 20 - 24 years
   - (9) 25 or more years

6. How long have you been a principal in this school, including this current year?
   - (1) One year
   - (2) Two years
   - (3) Three years
   - (4) 4 - 5 years
   - (5) 6 - 8 years
   - (6) 9 - 11 years
   - (7) 12 - 14 years
   - (8) 15 - 17 years
   - (9) 18 or more years

7. Which of the following best describes the college or university where you did your undergraduate work? *Choose only one answer.*
   - (1) Public university or college
   - (2) Private university or college, religiously affiliated
   - (3) Private university or college, not religiously affiliated
   - (4) Other: _____

8. What is your major field of <u>graduate</u> study? *Choose only one answer.*
   - (01) Educational administration and supervision
   - (02) Secondary education, curriculum and instruction
   - (03) Elementary education, curriculum and instruction
   - (04) Guidance and counseling
   - (05) Physical education
   - (06) Some other educational specialty: _____
   - (07) Humanities, social sciences, or fine arts
   - (08) Math or sciences
   - (09) Business
   - (10) Other: _____
   - (11) No graduate study

9. Which of the following <u>best</u> represents your administrative certification for the principalship.

   Choose only one answer.

   (1) Secondary
   (2) Middle
   (3) Elementary
   (4) No building level certification
   (5) Other: _____

10. What was the last position you held prior to becoming a middle level principal?

    Select only one answer.

    (01) Elementary teacher
    (02) Middle level teacher
    (03) High school teacher
    (04) Assistant principal of an elementary school
    (05) Assistant principal of a middle level school
    (06) Assistant principal of a high school
    (07) Principal of an elementary school
    (08) Principal of a high school
    (09) Guidance counselor
    (10) Central office administrator
    (11) College administrator or instructor
    (12) Other, education, specify: _____
    (13) Other, noneducation, specify: _____

11. How many years did you serve in your last position prior to becoming a middle level principal?

    (1) One year
    (2) 2 - 3 years
    (3) 4 - 5 years
    (4) 6 - 8 years
    (5) 8 - 9 years
    (6) 10 or more years

12. What is your current annual salary? Do not consider fringe benefits.

    (1) Less than $10,000
    (2) $10,000 - $14,999
    (3) $15,000 - $19,999
    (4) $20,000 - $24,999
    (5) $25,000 - $29,999
    (6) $30,000 - $34,999
    (7) $35,000 - $39,999
    (8) $40,000 - $44,999
    (9) $45,000 or more

13. Regardless of schedule of payment, is your yearly salary contract based upon:

    (1) 12 months
    (2) 11½ months
    (3) 11 months
    (4) 10½ months
    (5) 10 months
    (6) 9½ months
    (7) 9 months

14. Do you have tenure <u>as a principal</u>?   (1) Yes   (2) No

A4

15. Do you hope to move eventually to another position in the profession of education?
   - (01) Yes, to a middle level principalship in a larger district.
   - (02) Yes, to a middle level principalship in a smaller district.
   - (03) Yes, to a high school principalship.
   - (04) Yes, to an elementary school principalship.
   - (05) Yes, to a superintendency or central office position.
   - (06) Yes, to a junior college, college, or university position.
   - (07) Yes, to some other position, specify: _____
   - (08) I am undecided.
   - (09) No, I hope to remain in my present position.
   - (10) No, I hope to take a position outside the profession of education.

16. In how many civic and political organizations (Chamber of Commerce, Rotary Club, etc.) do you presently hold active membership?

   (1) None   (2) One   (3) Two   (4) Three   (5) Four   (6) Five or more

   For the next three questions, circle the number on line A which describes your perception of how your job actually is; circle the number on line B to describe how you think your job should be.

17. A. How much prestige do you feel your position as principal provides you in the community where your school is located?

1	2	3	4	5
Little		Moderate		Much

   B. How much prestige do you feel your position as principal should provide you in the community where your school is located?

1	2	3	4	5
Little		Moderate		Much

18. A. How much opportunity for independent thought and action <u>does</u> your position as principal provide?

1	2	3	4	5
Little		Moderate		Much

   B. How much opportunity for independent thought and action <u>should</u> your position as principal provide?

1	2	3	4	5
Little		Moderate		Much

19. A. How much self-fulfillment (i.e., the feeling of being able to use one's unique capabilities or realizing one's potential) <u>does</u> your position as principal provide?

1	2	3	4	5
Little		Moderate		Much

   B. How much self-fulfillment <u>should</u> your position as principal provide?

1	2	3	4	5
Little		Moderate		Much

20. How do you spend your time during the typical work week? Rank these nine areas according to the amount of time spent in each area.

In Column A, mark a "1" next to the area in which you do spend the most time, ranking all areas until you have marked a "9" next to the area in which you spend the least time.

Then, in Column B, mark a "1" next to the area in which you feel you should spend the most time, ranking all items accordingly until you have marked a "9" next to the area in which you feel you should spend the least time.

A. DO Spend Time	Area of Responsibility	SHOULD Spend Time
_____	Program Development (curriculum, instructional leadership, etc.)	_____
_____	Personnel (evaluating, advising, conferring, recruiting, etc.)	_____
_____	School Management (weekly calendar, office, budget, memos, etc.)	_____
_____	Student Activities (meetings, supervision, planning, etc.)	_____
_____	Student Behavior (discipline, attendance, meetings, etc.)	_____
_____	Community (PTA, advisory groups, parent conferences, etc.)	_____
_____	District Office (meetings, task forces, reports, etc.)	_____
_____	Professional Development (reading, conferences, etc.)	_____
_____	Planning (annual, long range)	_____

21. How much authority do you have to fill teacher vacancies? *Select one.*

    (1) I make the selection and the central office endorses it.

    (2) I make the selection within limited options stipulated by the central office.

    (3) I recommend a person to fill the vacancy and the central office makes the decision.

    (4) The central office selects the teacher to fill the vacancy.

22. To what extent do you participate in determining the budget allocation for your school?

    (1) High participation

    (2) Moderate participation

    (3) Little participation

    (4) No participation

23. It is important to have an understanding of the role of various individuals or groups in the decision-making process at the building level. Consider the types of decision in the left-hand column and then place a number for the individuals or groups listed across the top. Place 1 in the cell to indicate those who participate in deliberation about the decision; place a 2 for those who make recommendations; place a 3 for those who participate in making the actual decision.

Thus: 0 = No involvement   2 = Make recommendations
       1 = Involved in discussion   3 = Make decision

	Principal	Central Office Administration	Asst. Principal or Equivalent	Department Chairperson	Teachers (Individually)	Teachers as a group, committees, or faculty	Students	Parents and/or Community	School Board
A. Adding a new course or instructional program									
B. Adopting rules for student behavior									
C. Evaluating the school's grading practices									
D. Identifying or providing for areas of inservice									
E. Formulating school goals									
F. Developing a budget for your school									
G. Hiring of teaching staff									
H. Evaluating teaching staff									

24. What percent of your full-time teachers are women?

    (01) Less than 10%   (05) 40 - 49%   (09) 80 - 89%
    (02) 10 - 19%   (06) 50 - 59%   (10) 90 - 100%
    (03) 20 - 29%   (07) 60 - 69%
    (04) 30 - 39%   (08) 70 - 79%

25. Is the professional certification of the majority of your teachers:

    (1) Secondary   (2) Middle level   (3) Elementary

26. According to your best estimate, what percentage of your regular teachers did their student teaching at the middle level?

    (1) 25% or less   (2) 26 - 50%   (3) 51 - 75%   (4) 76 - 100%

27. In what manner has teacher salary influenced your ability to develop a well-qualified staff?

    (1) Low salaries have been a detriment to securing the better teachers.
    (2) High salaries have been an asset to securing the better teachers.
    (3) Salary has not been an influence in securing the better teachers.

A concern of middle level education has always been the number of teachers who leave middle level education for teaching positions in elementary or high schools. In your opinion, what percentage of the teachers in your building are committed to teaching at the middle level as contrasted to those who are awaiting the opportunity to take a position at another level of education.

(1) 25% or less   (2) 26 - 50%   (3) 51 - 75%   (4) 76 - 100%

How many students were enrolled in your school as of October 1, 1979?

(01) Less than 200   (05) 800 - 999   (09) 1600 - 1799
(02) 200 - 399   (06) 1000 - 1199   (10) 1800 - 1999
(03) 400 - 599   (07) 1200 - 1399   (11) 2000 or more
(04) 600 - 799   (08) 1400 - 1599

In your school, what is the classroom teacher to pupil ratio for the 1979-80 school year? Select the one alternative that comes closest to your ratio.

(1) 1 teacher for 10 or less students   (5) 1 teacher for 26 to 30 students
(2) 1 teacher for 11 to 15 students   (6) 1 teacher for 31 to 35 students
(3) 1 teacher for 16 to 20 students   (7) 1 teacher for 36 to 40 students
(4) 1 teacher for 21 to 25 students   (8) 1 teacher for 41 or more students

Which of the following population categories best describes the locality of the middle level school of which you are principal?

(1) City, more than 1,000,000
(2) City, 150,000 to 999,999
(3) Suburban, related to city of 150,000 population or more
(4) City, 25,000 to 149,999 population distinct from a metro area
(5) City, 5,000 to 24,999, not suburban
(6) Town or rural under 4,999

In which geographical region is your school located?

(1) New England   (4) Midwest   (7) West Coast
(2) Mid-Atlantic   (5) Southwest   (8) Alaska or Hawaii
(3) South   (6) Rocky Mountain Region

Much is written about involving parents and other citizens in education. Please identify the area(s) in which you involve parents or other citizens in a planning or advisory capacity in your school. *Circle all appropriate responses.*

(1) Objectives and priorities for the school
(2) Program changes and new programs being considered
(3) Student activities
(4) Student behavior, rights, responsibilities
(5) Finance and fund raising
(6) Evaluation of programs
(7) Evaluation of personnel
(8) General administration
(9) Parents are not involved in any of the above.

34. Listed below are community groups which may have sought, successfully or unsuccessfully, to bring about changes in the operation of your school. Place an "X" in the box which best indicates the extent of influence of each interest group on your school during the past two years.

INTEREST GROUP	Little/No Influence	Moderate Influence	Extreme Influence
A. Censorship groups (books, programs, etc.)			
B. Citizen or parent groups (non-PTA)			
C. Extreme left-wing individuals/groups			
D. Extreme right-wing individuals/groups			
E. Individuals/groups concerned about national reports, studies, etc.			
F. Legal aid groups			
G. Local elementary schools			
H. Local high schools			
I. Local labor organizations			
J. Local media (editorial policy)			
K. PTA or PTO			
L. Religious or church organizations			
M. State colleges and/or universities			
N. Teachers' association			
O. The business community			
P. Women's rights or minority organizations			
Q. Other:			

35. Which of the following categories best describes the middle level school of which you are principal. *Select only one.*

    (1) Public
    (2) Parochial or diocesan
    (3) Private, religious affiliated
    (4) Private, not religious affiliated
    (5) Other: _____

36. What grades are included in the middle level school of which you are principal?

    (01) 7-8-9   (03) 5-6-7   (05) 6-7-8-9   (07) 6-7   (09) 8-9
    (02) 6-7-8   (04) 5-6-7-8   (06) 5-6   (08) 7-8   (10) Other: _____

37. For how many years has your school operated under the current organizational structure; i.e., 7-8-9, or 5-6-7-8, or 7-8, or etc.

    (1) Less than 1 year   (4) 11 - 15 years   (7) 26 - 30 years
    (2) 1 - 5 years   (5) 16 - 20 years   (8) 31 - 50 years
    (3) 6 - 10 years   (6) 21 - 25 years   (9) Over 50 years

38. Which of the following describes the age in years of the physical plant (school building) in which you operate your school? Use the age of the original building, not the age of additions or remodeled sections.

    (1) Less than 5 years   (3) 11-15 years   (5) 21-25 years   (7) 31-50 years
    (2) 5-10 years   (4) 16-20 years   (6) 26-30 years   (8) Over 50 years

39. Does your middle level school use data processing machines for scheduling, record keeping or grade reporting? *Circle all of the appropriate responses.*

    (1) No, we do not have access to data process machines
    (2) Yes, we use them for scheduling
    (3) Yes, we use them for record keeping
    (4) Yes, we use them for grade reporting

Listed below are content areas often associated with middle level curriculum. Mark an "X" in the boxes for those grade levels in your school in which these content areas are a <u>required</u> part of the curriculum.

Content Area	Grade 5	Grade 6	Grade 7	Grade 8	Grade 9
English/Language Arts					
Mathematics					
Science					
Social Science					
Reading					
Physical Education					
Health					
Foreign Language					
Spelling					
Typing					
Art					
Crafts					
Home Economics					
Industrial Arts					
Speech					
Drama					
Photography					
General Music					
Vocal Music					
Chorus					
Instrumental Music					
Orchestra					
Career Education					
Other:					

Below are the content areas listed in the previous question. Please mark an "X" for the grades at which these content areas are an <u>elective</u> part of the curriculum.

Content Area	Grade 5	Grade 6	Grade 7	Grade 8	Grade 9
English/Language Arts					
Mathematics					
Science					
Social Science					
Reading					
Physical Education					
Health					
Foreign Language					
Spelling					
Typing					
Art					
Crafts					
Home Economics					
Industrial Arts					
Speech					
Drama					
Photography					
General Music					
Vocal Music					
Chorus					
Instrumental Music					
Orchestra					
Career Education					
Other:					

42. Below are four typical formats by which subjects are taught in schools. In your opinion, what approximate percent of time does a typical student in your school spend in each of these organizational formats. Indicate for those grade levels in your building only. Your responses for each grade should total 100%.

		Example	5	6	7	8	9	Non-Graded
A.	One subject taught by one teacher	40%						
B.	Several subjects taught by one teacher (self-contained classroom)	0%						
C.	One subject taught by a team of two or more teachers (subject area teams)	40%						
D.	Several subjects taught by a team of two or more teachers (interdisciplinary teaming)	20%						
	Total percent	100%	100%	100%	100%	100%	100%	100%

If other, please describe here: _____

43. Which one of the statements below best describes your school's operating policy toward "ability" grouping of pupils for instruction? If you do not ability group, circle (6)

   (1) Grouping is carried out at all grade levels and in all subject areas.
   (2) Grouping is carried out at all grade levels, but is restricted to certain subject areas.
   (3) Grouping is carried out at only certain grade levels, but the grouping is done in all subject areas at those levels.
   (4) Grouping is carried out only at certain grade levels and is restricted to certain subject areas at those levels.
   (5) We have a grouping system different from the alternatives above. Describe: _____
   (6) We do not have ability grouping.

44. If you have a program for the gifted or talented, what criteria are used to identify the students?

   (1) No gifted/talented program   (4) Teacher recommendations
   (2) Grades (G.P.A.)   (5) Standardized tests
   (3) Student interest   (6) Other: _____

45. Does your school have regularly scheduled parent conferences?

   (1) No   (2) Yes, 1-2 per year   (3) Yes, 3 or more per year

46. What was the average per pupil expenditure (exclusive of capital outlay) for each student in your school during the 1979-80 school year?

   (1) Less than $500   (5) $1500 - $1799
   (2) $500 - $899   (6) $1800 - $2099
   (3) $900 - $1199   (7) $2100 - $2399
   (4) $1200 - $1499   (8) $2400 or more

A11

. All things considered (learning conditions, teaching staff, capital outlay, etc.), what is your judgment about the optimum number of students for a middle level school? In deciding, focus on the 1979-80 school year.

(01) Less than 200
(02) 200 - 399
(03) 400 - 599
(04) 600 - 799
(05) 800 - 999
(06) 1000 - 1199
(07) 1200 - 1399
(08) 1400 - 1599
(09) 1600 - 1799
(10) 1800 - 1999
(11) 200 or more

. Would you be in favor of some system of individualized promotion for students rather than the customary use of grade placement and year-end promotion.

(1) Yes   (2) Yes, we have such a system   (2) No

. Based upon your experience, what do you think should be done about "ability" grouping policy for a middle level school?

(1) Ability grouping in all grade levels and all subject areas.
(2) Ability grouping in all grade levels, but restricted to certain subject areas.
(3) Ability grouping in only certain grade levels but in all subject areas at these levels.
(4) Ability grouping in only certain grade levels and restricted to certain subject areas at these levels.
(5) There should be a system of ability grouping different from the alternatives described above; please describe briefly:

_____

(6) There should be no ability grouping.

. Is your school accredited by a regional accrediting association? (1) Yes   (2) No

. Listed below are sports often associated with middle level education. For the appropriate sports, place an "X" in the spaces which correspond to the grade level and the sex of the students whom you feel should be given the opportunity to participate in interscholastic competition (between schools). We are interested in your opinion at all grade levels, not only for those levels in your own building.

SPORT	Grade 5 Boys	Grade 5 Girls	Grade 6 Boys	Grade 6 Girls	Grade 7 Boys	Grade 7 Girls	Grade 8 Boys	Grade 8 Girls	Grade 9 Boys	Grade 9 Girls
No interscholastic sports										
Football										
Basketball										
Baseball										
Softball										
Track										
Wrestling										
Swimming										
Gymnastics										
Tennis										
Volleyball										
Soccer										
Ice Hockey										
Other:										

A12

52. Identify the degree to which you feel the following <u>personal</u> characteristics of middle level teachers are important to the success of the teacher.
Mark an "X" in the appropriate box.

Characteristic	Not Important	Important	Very Important
Able to interact constructively with students and peers			
Able to work with students and bring out students' best capabilities			
Be a good model			
Committed to education of early adolescents			
Flexible			
Positive self-concept			
Respect the dignity and worth of the individual			
Sensitive to cultural heritage of students			
Sensitive to socio-economic background of the students			
Understand the students' skills, abilities, and interests			

53. Listed below are several reasons why middle level teachers might desire a change to teaching positions at the elementary or high school levels. Assign a rank of 1 to the reason you think might most strongly motivate such a teacher transfer, a rank of 2 to the second most significant reason, etc., until you assign a rank of 8 to the reason you consider least significant.

_____ Better facilities available elsewhere
_____ Desire to work with a different aged student
_____ Lack of adequate preparation to teach at middle level
_____ Lack of status and/or recognition at the middle level
_____ More money
_____ More preparation time
_____ Pupil-teacher ratio more attractive at other level
_____ Subject matter interest can be better met at other level

54. What do you think would be the ideal grade organizational structure for a middle level school?

(01) 7-8-9   (04) 5-6-7-8   (07) 6-7   (10) Other:
(02) 6-7-8   (05) 6-7-8-9   (08) 7-8   _____
(03) 5-6-7   (06) 5-6   (09) 8-9

55. What is your view of the role of special education in our middle level schools of today?

(1) Should be an integral part of the entire program.
(2) Important as a supplemental program for selected students.
(3) Unnecessary or inappropriate.

NATIONAL ASSOCIATION OF SECONDARY SCHOOL PRINCIPALS
Reston, Virginia 22091

A NATIONAL STUDY OF SCHOOLS IN THE MIDDLE

Survey of Middle Level Principals   (Form B)

Supported by the Geraldine R. Dodge Foundation

DIRECTIONS

Your questionnaire is identified by the label placed on it. It is not necessary to sign or place your name on the questionnaire. In reporting results, only statistical summaries of the responses of groups of principals will be cited. In no case will the identity of an individual be divulged. You are urged to make every answer a sincere one.

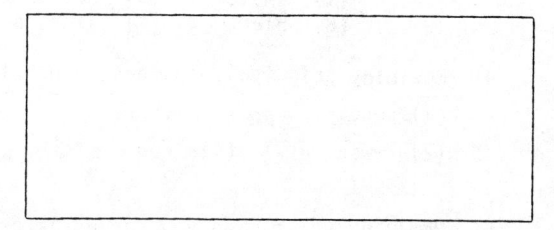

Circle the number of the appropriate response using pen or pencil. If you change a response, please make the change distinctly so there is no doubt about how you wish to answer.

Attempt to answer every question. For some questions none of the alternatives may correspond exactly to your situation or to the opinion you hold. In such cases mark the alternative which comes closest to the answer you would like to give.

For the purposes of this study, two terms should be clarified:

(1) *Middle level of education* is a general phrase used to encompass various combinations of grades five through nine.

(2) *Principal* refers to the chief building administrator and should not be confused with the role of assistant principal or vice principal, unless specifically stated.

Place your completed questionnaire in the envelope provided and mail it to NASSP. Thank you for your cooperation and assistance in this important study.

Steering Committee for the Study of Schools in the Middle:

Donald A. Stokes, King Junior High School, Portland, Maine; Kenneth M. Brashear, Comstock Middle School, Dallas, Tex.; Eugene B. Jump, Morgan Junior High School, Ellensburg, Wash.; Will Ella Brown, King Middle School, Dorchester, Mass.; Tom Maglaras, Aurora, Colo., Schools; Robert Mills, Central Michigan University.

Research Team:

Jerry Valentine, University of Missouri; Neal C. Nickerson, Jr., University of Minnesota; Anthony Gregorc, University of Connecticut; James W. Keefe, NASSP.

B2

1. What is your sex? (1) Male (2) Female

2. What is your age?
   (1) 23 or under
   (2) 24 - 29
   (3) 30 - 34
   (4) 35 - 39
   (5) 40 - 44
   (6) 45 - 49
   (7) 50 - 54
   (8) 55 - 59
   (9) 60 or older

3. With what ethnic group would you identify yourself?
   (1) White
   (2) Black
   (3) Chicano/Hispanic
   (4) American Indian
   (5) Asian
   (6) Other: _____

4. How many principalships have you held, including your present job?
   (1) One
   (2) Two
   (3) Three
   (4) Four
   (5) Five
   (6) Six
   (7) Seven
   (8) Eight or more

5. How many years have you served as a principal, including this current year?
   (1) One year
   (2) 2 - 3 years
   (3) 4 - 5 years
   (4) 6 - 7 years
   (5) 8 - 9 years
   (6) 10 - 14 years
   (7) 15 - 19 years
   (8) 20 - 24 years
   (9) 25 or more years

6. In which of the following areas did you major as an <u>undergraduate</u>? *Select only one answer.*
   (01) Secondary education (other than physical education)
   (02) Physical education
   (03) Elementary education
   (04) Humanities (literature, languages, etc.)
   (05) Physical or biological sciences
   (06) Social sciences (sociology, history, etc.)
   (07) Mathematics
   (08) Fine arts
   (09) Business
   (10) Vocational-Technical (home economics, industrial arts, etc.)
   (11) Other: _____

7. What is the highest degree you have earned?
   (01) Less than a BA
   (02) Bachelor's Degree
   (03) Master's Degree in Education
   (04) Master's Degree not in education
   (05) Master's Degree plus some additional graduate work
   (06) Educational Specialist, six-year program or equivalent
   (07) Master's Degree plus <u>all course work</u> for a doctorate
   (08) Doctor of Education
   (09) Doctor of Philosophy
   (10) Other: _____

8. Which of the following <u>best</u> represents your administrative certification for the principalship? *Choose only one answer.*
   (1) Secondary
   (2) Middle
   (3) Elementary
   (4) No building level certification
   (5) Other: _____

How many years of <u>teaching</u> experience, regardless of level, did you have prior to taking your present position? Do not include years as a full-time administrator or supervisor.

(1) None
(2) 1 year
(3) 2 - 3 years
(4) 4 - 6 years
(5) 7 - 9 years
(6) 10 - 14 years
(7) 15 - 19 years
(8) 20 - 24 years
(9) 25 or more years

What is your current annual salary? Do not consider fringe benefits.

(1) Less than $10,000
(2) $10,000 - $14,999
(3) $15,000 - $19,999
(4) $20,000 - $24,999
(5) $25,000 - $29,999
(6) $30,000 - $34,999
(7) $35,000 - $39,999
(8) $40,000 - $44,999
(9) $45,000 or more

What is the basis for your salary determination?

(1) Tied to a percentage of a step in the teacher salary schedule.
(2) My level in the teacher salary schedule plus an increment for administration.
(3) Negotiations are held for administration separate of teacher negotiations.
(4) Negotiated on an individual basis.
(5) Based upon a non-negotiated administrative salary schedule.
(6) Does not apply (religious order).
(7) Other: _____

Do you teach any regularly scheduled classes?

(1) No   (2) Yes - one course   (3) Yes - two or more courses

If you could choose again, would you select educational administration as a career?

(1) Yes - definitely
(2) Yes - probably
(3) Uncertain
(4) No - probably not
(5) No - definitely not

To what extent have you participated in the following activities during the past two years?

Mark and "X" in the appropriate boxes.

ACTIVITY	Very Extensively	Extensively	Slightly	Not At All
A. Studied at higher educational institutions (summer school, extension courses, evening classes, etc.)				
B. Participated in activities of professional associations (local, state, regional, national)				

B4

For the next three questions, circle the number on line A which describes your perception of how your job actually is; circle the number on line B as you think your job should be.

15. A. How much job security do you feel you have as a principal?

1	2	3	4	5
Little		Moderate		Much

    B. How much job security do you feel you should have as a principal?

1	2	3	4	5
Little		Moderate		Much

16. A. How much opportunity to be helpful to other people does your job as principal provide?

1	2	3	4	5
Little		Moderate		Much

    B. How much opportunity to be helpful to other people should your position as principal provide?

1	2	3	4	5
Little		Moderate		Much

17. A. How much self-fulfillment (i.e., the feeling of being able to use one's unique capabilities, or realizing one's potential) does your position as principal provide?

1	2	3	4	5
Little		Moderate		Much

    B. How much self-fulfillment should your position as principal provide?

1	2	3	4	5
Little		Moderate		Much

18. During the school year, on the average, how many hours a week do you work at your job as principal?

    (1) Less than 40
    (2) 40 - 49 hours
    (3) 50 - 59 hours
    (4) 60 - 69 hours
    (5) 70 or more hours

19. How much authority do you have to make personnel decisions such as employing one full-time teacher or an alternative; e.g., two or three teacher aides?

    (1) Unrestricted authority
    (2) Authority with some restriction
    (3) Little authority
    (4) No authority

20. To what extent do you have the authority to approve the allocation of discretionary funds within your school budget; i.e., how much autonomy or latitude do you have in the allocation of monies which are available to your building?

    (1) Unrestricted authority
    (2) Authority with some restriction
    (3) Little authority
    (4) No authority

1. Listed below are several factors which could be considered as "roadblocks" preventing principals from doing the job they would like to do. Using the alternatives below, indicate by marking an "X" in the appropriate boxes whether each factor has or has not been a roadblock to you as principal over the past two years.

FACTOR	Not a Factor	Somewhat a Factor	Serious Factor
Collective bargaining agreement			
Defective communication among administrative levels			
Inability to obtain funding			
Inability to provide teacher time for planning or professional development			
Insufficient space and physical facilities			
Lack of competent administrative assistance			
Lack of competent office help			
Lack of district-wide flexibility (all schools conform to same policy)			
Lack of knowledge among staff regarding programs for middle level students			
Lack of time for myself			
Long-standing tradition in the school/district			
Parents apathetic or irresponsible about their children			
Pressure from community			
Problem students (apathetic, hostile, etc.)			
Resistance to change by staff			
Superintendent or central office staff who have not measured up to expectations			
Teacher tenure			
Teacher turnover			
Time required to administer, supervise extracurricular activities			
Time taken by administrative detail at expense of more important matters			
Too large a student body			
Too small a student body			
Variations in the ability and dedication of staff			

2. What level of education is most representative of teachers new to your school within the past five years?

(1) Less than 4-yr. degree   (3) Master's degree   (5) Ed.D. or Ph.D.
(2) Bachelor's degree   (4) Master's degree + addl. grad. hours

3. In recent years, the issue of teacher preparation has been a topic of much interest. Which of the following best describe the method(s) by which your teachers have been prepared to teach, specifically, at the middle level?
(*Circle more than one if appropriate.*)

(1) Inservice programs
(2) Preschool workshops
(3) Student/practice teaching at middle level
(4) Courses at the university which focus on middle level education
(5) Personal or self-study
(6) Other: _____
(7) Generally, the staff has not had special preparation to teach at the middle level.

4. Does your middle level school cooperate with a teacher training institution by providing teaching experiences for future teachers?

                (1) Yes   (2) No

B6

25. Circle the number which most nearly corresponds to the number of full-time equivalent (FTE) personnel you have for each position listed. (Two half-time personnel would be equal to one full-time person, 2-3/4 FTE to three, etc.)

PERSONNEL						
Assistant Principal or equivalent personnel	0	1	2	3	4	5+
Librarian/Media Specialist	0	1	2	3	4	5+
Office Secretaries/Clerks	0	1	2	3	4	5+
Instructional Aides	0	1	2	3	4	5+
Nurses	0	1	2	3	4	5+
Counselors	0	1	2	3	4	5+
Special Education Teachers	0	1	2	3	4	5+
Security/Supervisory Aides	0	1	2	3	4	5+

26. For this question, please circle the number on the line which describes your perception of the quantity and quality of your administrative staff.

   A. The amount of administrative assistance in my building is:

1	2	3	4	5
Inadequate		Adequate		More than adequate

   B. The quality of administrative assistance in my building is:

1	2	3	4	5
Inadequate		Adequate		More than adequate

27. How many students were enrolled in your school as of October 1, 1979?

   (01) Less than 200   (4) 600-799   (07) 1200-1399   (10) 1800-1999
   (02) 200-399   (05) 800-999   (08) 1400-1599   (11) 2000 or more
   (03) 400-599   (06) 1000-1199   (09) 1600-1799

28. What do you estimate to be the percent of average daily attendance of those enrolled in your school during the 1979-80 school year?

   (1) Less than 50%   (3) 61 - 70%   (5) 81 - 90%   (07) 96% or more
   (2) 51 - 60%   (4) 71 - 80%   (6) 91 - 95%

29. Which of the following population categories best describes the locality of the middle level school of which you are principal?

   (1) City, more than 1,000,000
   (2) City, 150,000 to 999,999
   (3) Suburban, related to city of 150,000 population or more
   (4) City, 25,000 to 149,999 population distinct from a metro area
   (5) City, 5,000 to 24,999, not suburban
   (6) Town or rural under 4,999

30. In which geographical region is your middle level school located?

   (1) New England   (5) Southwest
   (2) Mid-Atlantic   (6) Rocky Mountain Region
   (3) South   (7) Alaska or Hawaii
   (4) Midwest

31. In your opinion what is occurring with regard to parent, citizen, and student involvement in your school? Use this present school year as the basis for your response.

   A. The desire of parents to participate is
      (1) increasing over previous years.
      (2) decreasing from previous years.
      (3) remaining about the same as in previous years.

   B. The desire of citizens other than parents to participate is
      (1) increasing over previous years.
      (2) decreasing from previous years.
      (3) remaining about the same as in previous years.

   C. The desire of students to participate is
      (1) increasing over previous years.
      (2) decreasing from previous years.
      (3) remaining about the same as in previous years.

32. Please circle all the areas in which you involve parents or other citizens in the operation of your school.

   (1) Advisors, counselors to individual students
   (2) Monitors, supervisors, ticket sellers, etc., of student activities
   (3) Operators of concessions, etc., for the benefit of the school
   (4) Resource persons to programs and activities, including instruction
   (5) Sponsors/moderators of student groups
   (6) Volunteer aides
   (7) Volunteer tutors
   (8) Other: _____

33. Which of the following categories best describes the middle level school of which you are principal. *Select only one.*

   (1) Public
   (2) Parochial or diocesan
   (3) Private, religious affiliated
   (4) Private, not religious affiliated
   (5) Other: _____

34. What grades are included in the middle level school of which you are principal?

   (01) 7-8-9   (03) 5-6-7   (05) 6-7-8-9   (07) 6-7   (09) 8-9
   (02) 6-7-8   (04) 5-6-7-8   (06) 5-6   (08) 7-8   (10) Other: _____

35. If your school has adopted a "middle school" organizational plan which includes either grades 5-6-7-8 or 6-7-8, please circle all the reason(s) for adopting either of these two patterns. If your system has not changed to a middle school plan of grades 5-6-7-8 or 6-7-8, please circle item (10).

   (01) To provide a better transition from elementary to high school
   (02) To solve concerns about a junior high program
   (03) To employ new curriculum or instructional innovations
   (04) To utilize a new school facility or building
   (05) To adjust to enrollment trends
   (06) To employ ideas or programs successfully implemented in other schools
   (07) To provide a program best suited to the needs of the middle level age child
   (08) To move ninth graders into a high school program
   (09) To provide fifth and/or sixth graders with more curricular specialization
   (10) Does not apply.

36. Is your middle level school housed in a separate building; i.e., is the actual physical plant located in a different building from that of a local elementary or high school?

　　　　　　　　　　(1)　Yes　　　　　　　(2)　No

37. Place an "X" in the box beside each of the following facilities which are available in your middle level school.

FACILITY

(A)	Gymnasium	
(B)	Library	
(C)	Instructional Materials Center	
(D)	Media Center	
(E)	Industrial Arts Lab	
(F)	Mathematics Lab	
(G)	Reading Lab	
(H)	Social Science Lab	
(I)	Language Lab	
(J)	Music Room	
(K)	Art Room	
(L)	Crafts Room	
(M)	Computer or data processing facility	

38. Indicate the federal or state programs for which your school has received funding in the past three years.　　*Circle all appropriate responses.*

    (01) Federal Title I (ESEA)
    (02) State Compensatory Education
    (03) Vocational Education
    (04) Impact Aid
    (05) Career Education
    (06) Special Education
    (07) Bilingual Education
    (08) Assistance to Indo-Chinese Refugee Children
    (09) Desegregation (Emergency School Aid Act)
    (10) Title IV (Instructional)
    (11) Title III or IVc (Innovative Programs)
    (12) Other: _____
    (13) No federal or state funding for the above programs in the past three years.

39. Which of the following best describes the typical format by which your students are grouped for instructional purposes? In your opinion, what approximate percent of time does a typical student in your school spend in each of these instructional groupings. Indicate for those grade levels in your building only. Your responses for each grade should total 100%.

G R A D E S

Groupings	Example	5	6	7	8	9	Non-Graded
A. Traditional class sizes (15-35 students)	80%						
B. Small group instruction (2-15 students)	10%						
C. Large group instruction (more than 35)	5%						
D. Individualized instruction	5%						
Total	100%	100%	100%	100%	100%	100%	100%

40. Identify the types of programs for which students in your school may enroll. *Circle all that apply.*

    (1) Courses taught at the high school
    (2) Credit by examination
    (3) Credit by contract or independent study
    (4) Off-campus work experience
    (5) Community volunteer programs
    (6) Summer school enrichment or remediation programs
    (7) Other: _____

41. If you use ability grouping, what criteria are being used for the purpose of grouping? *Circle all applicable responses.*

    (1) No ability grouping in our school
    (2) Grades
    (3) I.Q. scores
    (4) Judgments of school staff
    (5) Standardized achievement tests
    (6) Parental input
    (7) Performance/Criterion-referenced testing
    (8) Other: _____

42. Listed below are sports often associated with middle level education. For the appropriate sports, place an "X" in the spaces which correspond to the grade level and the sex of the students who are permitted to participate in <u>interscholastic competition</u> (between schools) in your school this year.

SPORT	Grade 5 Boys	Grade 5 Girls	Grade 6 Boys	Grade 6 Girls	Grade 7 Boys	Grade 7 Girls	Grade 8 Boys	Grade 8 Girls	Grade 9 Boys	Grade 9 Girls
No Interscholastic Sports										
Football										
Basketball										
Baseball										
Softball										
Track										
Wrestling										
Swimming										
Gymnastics										
Tennis										
Volleyball										
Soccer										
Ice Hockey										
Other:										

43. Listed below are extracurricular or cocurricular areas often associated with middle level education. For the appropriate activities, place an "X" in the spaces which correspond to the grade level and sex of the students who may participate in these activities at your school.

ACTIVITY	Grade 5 Boys	Grade 5 Girls	Grade 6 Boys	Grade 6 Girls	Grade 7 Boys	Grade 7 Girls	Grade 8 Boys	Grade 8 Girls	Grade 9 Boys	Grade 9 Girls
Intramural athletics										
Student government										
Student clubs										
Honor societies										
Dramatics										
Publications										
Musical groups										
Other:										

44. If you have a gifted and/or talented program in your school, which of the following describe the organizational format(s) of the program?

    Circle all appropriate responses.

    (1) No gifted/talented program
    (2) Released time during school hours (special class)
    (3) Regular class situation with individualized projects focusing specifically upon the gifted/talented
    (4) After school, evening, or weekend program
    (5) Summer program
    (6) Cooperative program with high school
    (7) Program offered in conjunction with district, region, or state department of education
    (8) Other: _____

45. The following items are concerned with administrative articulation of the middle level with both elementary and high school levels. Articulation is defined as the coordination of efforts between these levels. Considering the various alternatives, indicate whether you feel there is a problem of articulation in your setting.

    Please respond for both elementary and high school articulation by marking an "X" in the appropriate boxes.

AREA	ELEMENTARY ARTICULATION			SECONDARY ARTICULATION		
	Major Problem	Minor Problem	No Problem	Major Problem	Minor Problem	No Problem
A. Student records						
B. Pupil promotion policies						
C. Granting of subject credit						
D. Subject content and sequence						
E. Counseling services						
F. Marking/grading systems						

46. What was the average per pupil expenditure (exclusive of capital outlay) for each student in your school during the 1979-80 school year?

    (1) Less than $500   (3) $999 - $1199   (5) $1500 - $1799   (7) $2100 - $2399
    (2) $500 - $899   (4) $1200 - $1499   (6) $1800 - $2099   (8) $2400 or more

47. Some say the public schools should not make important curricular changes without first securing community support. What is your opinion of this issue?

    (1) Strongly agree   (3) Indifferent   (4) Disagree
    (2) Agree   (5) Strongly disagree

48. In your opinion, if class sizes are maintained at about their present levels, do technological advances (T.V., Computer Assisted Instruction, etc.) hold real promise for improving the quality of education in middle level schools?

    (1) Yes, considerable promise   (3) No, little if any promise
    (2) Yes, some promise   (4) No, would definitely be harmful

9. Do you favor systematic competency testing of basic skills for promotion?
   Circle only one response.
   (1) Yes   (3) Some advantages, some disadvantages
   (2) Yes, and we have such a system (4) No

10. Is your school accredited by a regional accreditation association?
    (1) Yes   (2) No

11. Identify any grade levels at which you feel greater emphasis should be placed upon intramural rather than interscholastic activities.
    (1) All middle level grades (5-6-7-8-9)
    (2) Grades eight and below   (5-6-7-8)
    (3) Grades seven and below   (5-6-7)
    (4) Grades six and below   (5-6)
    (5) Grade five   (5)

12. Identify the degree to which you feel the following <u>professional</u> characteristics of the middle level teacher are important to the success of the teacher.
    Mark an "X" in the appropriate box.

The ability to:	Not Important	Important	Very Important
Counsel students			
Promote independent learning among students			
Teach communication skills			
Use techniques of inquiry oriented problem solving			
Utilize multi-media approaches to instruction			
Use positive methods of classroom control			
Utilize values clarification activities appropriately			
Employ varied learning strategies (not merely lecture and recitation)			
Work across interdisciplinary lines			
Work as a member of a teaching team			

It is appropriate that the professional education of middle level teachers include "special courses geared to the middle level." *Please rank the following preservice areas.*

Assign a rank of "1" to the course work area below you consider most important in the preparation of middle level teachers, a rank of "2" to the next most important, until you assign a rank of "7" to the least important of the choices provided.

_____ Curriculum for the middle level
_____ Guidance/counseling for the middle level
_____ Psychology of the middle level student
_____ Student/practice teaching at the middle level
_____ Teaching methods for the middle level
_____ Teaching of reading
_____ The history, purposes, and functions of the middle level school

B12

54. Should principals have tenure as administrators?

   (1) Yes   (2) No

55. Much has been written about the tasks of American schools. Please rank the 11 statements below according to your belief about their relative importance as educational purposes.

Assign a rank of "1" to the statement you consider most important, a rank of "2" to the next most important, until you assign a rank of "11" to the statement you consider least important.

 _____ Acquisition of basic skills (reading, writing, speaking, computing, etc.)

 _____ Appreciation for and experience with the fine arts

 _____ Career planning and training in beginning occupational skills

 _____ Development of moral and spiritual values

 _____ Development of positive self-concept and good human relations

 _____ Development of skills and practice of critical intellectual inquiry and problem solving

 _____ Development of the skills to operate a technological society (engineering, scientific, etc.)

 _____ Knowledge about and skills in preparation for family life (e.g., sex education, home management, problems of aging, etc.)

 _____ Preparation for a changing world

 _____ Physical fitness and useful leisure time sports

 _____ Understanding of the American value system (its political, economic, social values, etc.)

APPENDIX B: SUPPLEMENTARY DATA

The following tables will be of interest to some researchers and practitioners. These supplementary tables are keyed to the primary tables in the text. Table 22A, for example, provides supplementary analysis of the information contained in Table 22 of the main body of this report.

22A	Number of Principalships by Sex
23A	Years in the Principalship by Enrollment
27A	Years as Principal in This School by Enrollment
36A	Undergraduate College by Region
39A	Major Field of Graduate Study by Region
43A	Highest Earned Degree by Region
47A	Administrative Certification by Region
49A	Salary by Grade Level
49B	Salary by School Enrollment
49C	Salary by Region
52A	Basis for Salary Determination by Region
53A	Length of Salary Contract by Region
53B	Length of Salary Contract by Grade Level
58A	Participation in Professional Activities by Sex
61A	Number of Civic and Political Organization Memberships by Sex
61B	Number of Civic and Political Organization Memberships by Population
61C	Number of Civic and Political Organization Memberships by Region
70A	Teaching Responsibilities by Enrollment
72A	Actual Prestige of Position by Enrollment
72B	Actual Prestige of Position by Region
76A	Authority in Staffing Practices by Grade Level
78A	Authority To Fill Teacher Vacancies by Grade Level
78B	Authority To Fill Teacher Vacancies by Population
84A	School Staff Full-Time Equivalents
91A	Enrollment Based upon Region of the U.S.
91B	Enrollment Based upon Community Population
91C	Enrollment Based upon Per-Pupil Expenditures
93A	Average Daily Attendance by Community Population
93B	Average Daily Attendance by Region of U.S.
102A	Region by Type of School
103A	Years in Current Grade Level Organization by Population
103B	Years in Current Grade Level Organization by Enrollment
105A	Years in Current Grade Level Organization by Region
105B	Years in Current Grade Level Organization by Population
107A	Average Per-Pupil Expenditure by Region
107B	Average Per-Pupil Expenditure by Population
108A	Types of Facilities by Region
112A	Required Courses and Electives by Grade Level Organization
118A	Scope of Ability Grouping by Population
118B	Scope of Ability Grouping by Enrollment
122A	Criteria for Admittance to Gifted Programs by Per-Pupil Expenditure
125A	Funded Programs by Population
126A	Interscholastic Sports for Boys by Population
127A	Interscholastic Sports for Girls by Population
132A	Data Processing by Enrollment
132B	Data Processing by Per-Pupil Expenditure
134A	Opinions About Ability Grouping Policies by Enrollment
135A	Opinions About the Role of Special Education in Middle School by Grade Level Organization

143A Opinions About the Ideal Middle Level Grade Organizational Structure by Population
143B Opinions About the Ideal Middle Level Grade Organizational Structure by Enrollment
146A Opinions About Optimal Number of Students for a Middle Level School by Population
151A Opinions Regarding Support for Administrative Tenure by Population
151B Opinions Regarding Support for Administrative Tenure by Enrollment

TABLE 22A
Number of Principalships by Sex

	Total	Male	Female
1	50	50	54
2	28	28	31
3	13	14	4
4	5	5	7
5	2	2	4
6	1	1	0
7	1	1	0
8	1	1	0

TABLE 23A
Years in the Principalship by Enrollment

	1980 Total	<400	400-599	600-799	800-999	1,000-1,399	1,400+
1	7	8	8	5	8	8	3
2-3	12	24	10	11	8	9	21
4-5	10	12	8	12	9	11	0
6-7	13	12	12	13	13	14	12
8-9	11	10	10	11	13	10	15
10-14	22	19	24	20	21	25	33
15-19	13	7	14	14	16	13	8
20-24	8	3	11	9	7	7	8
25+	4	5	3	5	5	3	0

TABLE 27A
Years as Principal in This School by Enrollment

	1980 Total	<400	400-599	600-799	800-999	1,000-1,399	1,400+
1	13	16	12	12	13	19	13
2	12	10	10	11	16	15	8
3	9	14	8	11	10	4	4
4-5	16	11	12	14	23	21	25
6-8	19	10	22	22	12	20	12
9-11	12	12	13	11	13	9	4
12-14	8	7	7	10	7	5	13
15-17	6	6	9	4	6	4	13
18+	5	4	7	5	0	3	8

TABLE 36A
Undergraduate College by Region

	1980 Total	New England	Middle Atlantic	South	Mid-west	South-west	Rocky Mountain	Far West
Public	69	53	64	65	75	73	81	82
Private-religious affiliated	23	24	20	28	21	25	13	15
Private—not religious affiliated	7	21	16	7	3	2	6	3
Other	1	2	0	0	1	0	0	0

TABLE 39A
Major Field of Graduate Study by Region

Graduate Major	1980 Total	New England	Middle Atlantic	South	Mid-west	South-west	Rocky Mountain	Far West
Educ. admin.	75	79	66	76	80	79	75	67
Sec. educ.	6	5	8	5	7	5	0	3
Elem. educ.	1	4	0	5	0	2	0	0
Guidance	5	4	6	4	6	3	3	8
Phys. educ.	2	0	1	2	1	3	3	4
Educ. spec.	2	2	2	2	1	3	0	0
Hum/SS/Arts	3	2	8	2	2	0	3	10
Math/Sci.	4	4	5	4	2	3	13	4
Business	<1	0	0	0	0	2	0	1
Other	1	0	3	0	1	0	3	3
None	<1	0	1	0	0	0	0	0

TABLE 43A
Highest Earned Degree by Region

	1980 Total	New England	Middle Atlantic	South	Mid-west	South-west	Rocky Mountain	Far West
Bachelor's	1	2	0	1	<1	2	3	12
Master's in educ.	23	13	11	27	23	32	11	26
Master's not educ.	1	2	2	1	<1	1	3	1
Masters +	49	48	56	40	50	54	65	40
Specialist	10	16	4	18	13	6	3	2
All but degree	7	9	19	4	5	3	5	12
Ed.D.	5	2	5	7	4	1	5	3
Ph.D.	3	3	1	1	3	1	5	4
Other	1	5	2	1	<1	0	0	<1

TABLE 47A
Administrative Certification by Region

	1980 Total	New England	Middle Atlantic	South	Mid-west	South-west	Rocky Mountain	Far West
Secondary	66	61	74	63	67	62	81	61
Middle	8	6	6	10	10	5	2	4
Elementary	7	8	3	5	9	5	7	14
No building level certification	6	9	3	12	5	10	1	11
Other	13	16	14	10	9	18	9	10

TABLE 49A
Salary by Grade Level

	1980 Total	7-8-9	7-8	6-7-8	5-6-7-8	Other
<$15,000	1	1	1	1	5	5
$15,000-$19,999	5	4	6	6	7	8
$20,000-$24,999	26	18	28	25	42	49
$25,000-$29,999	32	33	32	33	31	25
$30,000-$34,999	26	30	25	27	13	11
$35,000-$39,999	8	12	6	6	2	4
$40,000+	2	2	2	2	0	1

TABLE 49B
Salary by School Enrollment

	1980 Total	<400	400-599	600-799	800-999	1,000-1,399	1,400+
<$15,000	1	6	2	0	1	0	0
$15,000-$19,999	5	20	4	2	1	0	1
$20,000-$24,999	26	44	28	23	14	16	3
$25,000-$29,999	32	20	35	33	35	33	21
$30,000-$34,999	26	7	25	31	36	28	22
$35,000-$39,999	8	2	4	9	10	19	41
$40,000+	2	1	2	2	3	4	12

TABLE 49C
Salary by Region

	1980 Total	New England	Middle Atlantic	South	Mid-west	South-west	Rocky Mountain	Far West
<$15,000	1	3	1	2	1	0	0	1
$15,000-$19,999	5	4	3	10	4	9	9	1
$20,000-$24,999	26	24	14	48	24	40	23	3
$25,000-$29,999	32	37	27	34	35	38	34	18
$30,000-$34,999	26	21	26	5	29	12	25	60
$35,000-$39,999	8	9	20	1	7	1	9	12
$40,000+	2	2	9	0	0	0	0	5

TABLE 52A
Basis for Salary Determination by Region

	1980 Total	New England	Middle Atlantic	South	Midwest	Southwest	Rocky Mountain	Far West
Percentage of teacher	15	20	17	15	13	23	16	15
Teacher plus	15	9	10	36	9	35	3	11
Separate administrator negotiation	36	59	44	6	41	16	35	57
Individual negotiation	6	2	3	2	12	3	8	2
Nonnegotiated administrator schedule	23	2	21	38	18	22	30	14
DNA	1	3	1	1	0	0	0	1
Other	4	5	4	2	7	1	8	0

TABLE 53A
Length of Salary Contract by Region

Months	1980 Total	New England	Middle Atlantic	South	Midwest	Southwest	Rocky Mountain	Far West
12	47	58	75	63	33	29	29	39
11½	<1	0	0	1	1	0	0	4
11	28	19	18	22	32	50	23	26
10½	15	13	4	5	21	13	19	24
10	10	10	3	9	12	8	26	7
9½	<1	0	0	0	1	0	3	0
9	0	0	0	0	0	0	0	0

TABLE 53B
Length of Salary Contract by Grade Level

Months	1980 Total	7-8-9	7-8	6-7-8	5-6-7-8	Other
12	47	51	41	47	38	44
11	28	28	28	28	29	38
10½	15	13	18	11	14	11
10	10	8	13	14	19	7

TABLE 58A
Participation in Professional Activities by Sex

	1980 Total	Male	Female
Extensively	54	53	61
Little or none	46	47	39

TABLE 61A
Number of Civic and Political Organization Memberships by Sex

	1980 Total	Male	Female
None	34	36	19
One or more	66	64	81

TABLE 61B
Number of Civic and Political Organization Memberships by Population

	1980 Total	City of 150,000+	Suburban	25,000-149,999	5,000-24,999	Rural
None	34	46	40	28	26	32
One or more	66	54	60	72	74	68

TABLE 61C
Number of in Civic and Political Organization Memberships by Region

	1980 Total	New Engand	Mid. Atlantic	South	Midwest	Southwest	Rocky Mountain	Far West
None	34	57	32	33	26	34	23	44
One or more	66	43	68	67	74	66	77	56

TABLE 70A
Teaching Responsibilities by Enrollment

	1980 Total	<400	400-599	600-799	800-999	1,000-1,399	1,400+
None	96	68	99	99	100	99	100
One	2	10	1	1	0	1	0
Two +	2	22	0	0	0	0	0

TABLE 72A
Actual Prestige of Position by Enrollment

	1980 Total	<400	400-599	600-799	800-999	1,000-1,399	1,400+
1. (Little)	1	2	1	0	0	0	0
2.	4	6	5	4	2	5	0
3. (Moderate)	40	39	37	39	47	38	50
4.	42	43	46	41	33	43	46
5. (Much)	13	10	11	16	18	14	4

TABLE 72B
Actual Prestige of Position by Region

	1980 Total	New England	Middle Atlantic	South	Midwest	Southwest	Rocky Mountain	Far West
1. (Little)	1	0	1	1	0	0	0	0
2.	4	4	8	5	6	0	0	3
3. (Moderate)	40	30	43	46	39	51	48	30
4.	42	38	37	37	42	39	45	57
5. (Much)	13	28	11	11	13	10	7	10

TABLE 76A
Authority in Staffing Practices by Grade Level

	1980 Total	7-8-9	7-8	6-7-8	5-6-7-8	Other
Unrestricted	5	5	6	7	3	6
With some restrictions	62	59	63	59	76	61
Little	20	21	20	21	12	24
None	13	15	11	13	9	19

TABLE 78A
Authority To Fill Teacher Vacancies by Grade Level

	1980 Total	7-8-9	7-8	6-7-8	5-6-7-8	Other
Make decision	33	34	30	39	48	28
Limited	32	32	34	29	28	27
Recommend	26	24	29	20	24	38
Central office selects	9	10	7	12	0	7

TABLE 78B
Authority To Fill Teacher Vacancies by Population

	1980 Total	City of 150,000+	Suburban	25,000-149,999	5,000-24,999	Rural
Make decision	33	12	34	33	36	43
Limited	32	43	35	35	34	16
Recommend	26	20	25	27	26	29
Central office selects	9	25	6	5	4	12

TABLE 84A
School Staff Full-Time Equivalents

Position	1966	1980	1980 F.T.E.*
Assistant principal	42	77	1.0
Librarian/Media specialist	64	96	1.0
Counselors	61	90	1.7
Special education teachers	—	97	2.6
Instructional aides	—	78	2.2
Security/Supervisory aides	—	26	.5
Office secretaries/Clerks	76	99	2.5
Nurses	15	61	.6

*Includes schools with one or more full-time persons. F.T.E. represents average number of persons for all schools in the study.

TABLE 91A
Enrollment Based upon Region of the U.S.

	All Schools	New England	Middle Atlantic	South	Midwest	Southwest	Rocky Mountain	Far West
<400	20	24	11	14	24	29	22	21
400-599	25	23	23	23	30	19	25	29
600-799	24	24	28	28	24	18	21	28
800-999	18	16	20	18	15	22	19	21
1,000-1,399	10	13	14	15	5	12	12	14
1,400+	3	0	4	2	1	0	1	7

TABLE 91B
Enrollment Based upon Community Population

	All Schools	City of 150,000+	Suburban	25,000-149,999	5,000-24,999	Rural
<400	20	6	7	8	20	55
400-599	25	17	24	20	33	28
600-799	24	23	27	32	26	13
800-999	18	22	24	26	14	3
1,000-1,399	10	23	15	13	6	1
1,400+	3	9	3	1	1	0

TABLE 91C
Enrollment Based upon Per-Pupil Expenditure

	All Schools	<1,200	1,200-1,799	1,800+
<400	20	22	19	16
400-599	25	25	24	28
600-799	24	24	25	28
800-999	18	15	20	18
1,000-1,399	10	12	10	8
1,400+	3	2	2	2

TABLE 93A
Average Daily Attendance by Community Population

ADA	All Schools	City of 150,000+	Suburban	25,000-149,999	5,000-24,999	Rural
96+	19	10	23	15	16	31
91-95	60	42	67	64	65	57
81-90	18	36	9	20	17	11
<81	3	12	1	1	2	1

TABLE 93B
Average Daily Attendance by Region of U.S.

ADA	All Schools	New England	Middle Atlantic	South	Mid-West	South-West	Rocky Mountain	Far West
96+	19	21	13	16	24	13	11	24
91-95	60	59	68	56	61	67	65	54
81-90	18	20	14	25	14	17	24	16
<81	3	0	5	3	1	3	0	6

TABLE 102A
Region by Type of School

	Public	Parochial	Private Religious
New England	8	27	—
Middle Atlantic	14	9	29
South	18	9	43
Midwest	33	27	14
Southwest	10	—	—
Rocky Mountain	5	—	—
Far West	12	—	—

TABLE 103A
Years in Current Grade Level Organization by Population

	Total	7-8-9	7-8	6-7-8	5-6-7-8	Other
150,000+	13	18	9	9	4	9
Suburban	21	25	20	16	9	25
25,000-149,999	23	30	20	20	8	8
5,000-24,999	22	16	27	24	23	25
Rural	21	11	24	31	57	33

TABLE 103B
Years in Current Grade Level Organization by Enrollment

	Total	7-8-9	7-8	6-7-8	5-6-7-8	Other
<400	20	8	31	19	44	33
400-599	25	19	30	30	30	21
600-799	24	27	24	24	13	29
800-999	18	26	8	18	9	13
1,000-1,399	10	15	7	8	4	4
1,400+	3	5	<1	1	—	—

TABLE 105A
Years in Current Grade Level Organization by Region

Years	New England	Middle Atlantic	South	Midwest	Southwest	Rocky Mountain	Far West
0-5	21	20	23	14	32	16	14
6-10	36	20	40	21	28	19	20
11-15	21	22	23	19	15	10	17
16-20	9	19	5	19	10	19	15
21+	13	19	9	27	15	36	34

TABLE 105B
Years in Current Grade Level Organization by Population

Years	City of 150,000+	Suburban	25,000-149,999	5,000-24,999	Rural
0-5	21	20	15	20	19
6-10	18	24	24	29	32
11-15	10	21	16	19	24
16-20	11	21	10	16	14
21+	40	14	35	16	11

TABLE 107A
Average Per-Pupil Expenditure by Region

	New England	Middle Atlantic	South	Midwest	Southwest	Rocky Mountain	Far West
<$1,200	55	42	42	38	29	34	49
$1,200-1,799	26	37	44	46	49	45	33
$1,800+	19	21	14	16	22	21	18

TABLE 107B
Average Per-Pupil Expenditure by Population

	City of 150,000+	Suburban	25,000-149,999	5,000-24,999	Rural
<$1,200	41	21	38	43	45
$1,200-1,799	44	46	43	45	41
$1,800+	15	33	19	12	14

TABLE 108A
Types of Facilities by Region

	New England	Middle Atlantic	South	Midwest	Southwest	Rocky Mountain	Far West
Gymnasium	89	93	87	96	88	97	66
Library	93	88	92	91	94	92	92
I.M.C.	59	50	47	59	54	65	55
Media center	38	48	68	53	57	59	36
Industrial arts lab	79	84	68	85	72	86	78
Math lab	25	38	29	31	40	46	41
Reading lab	52	63	60	64	74	62	71
Social science lab	5	14	9	17	24	30	14
Language lab	14	25	26	29	36	43	26
Music room	80	89	88	96	94	97	88
Art room	82	91	77	93	86	94	84
Crafts room	34	37	35	44	53	70	63
Computer facility	21	19	18	23	20	27	26

TABLE 112A
Required Courses and Electives by Grade Level Organization

	7 R	7 E	8 R	8 E	9 R	9 E	7 R	7 E	8 R	8 E	6 R	6 E	7 R	7 E	8 R	8 E	5 R	5 E	6 R	6 E	7 R	7 E	8 R	8 E
English/Language arts	98	1	98	3	97	4	99	2	99	2	99	0	100	1	95	1	100	0	100	0	100	0	100	0
Math	98	1	97	3	93	9	100	2	99	2	99	0	99	1	97	2	100	0	100	0	100	0	100	0
Science	89	3	93	6	72	26	95	3	92	7	98	1	99	2	94	2	100	0	100	0	100	0	100	0
Social studies	96	0	96	3	82	17	97	3	95	5	96	0	99	1	88	1	90	0	90	0	90	0	81	0
Reading	63	24	48	30	26	34	81	15	71	20	95	1	79	10	70	12	100	0	90	0	81	0	81	0
Physical education	95	6	91	9	86	14	99	3	95	7	98	1	95	4	84	8	95	5	95	5	100	5	86	10
Health	55	4	50	6	36	9	72	5	60	7	78	1	70	0	60	1	76	0	81	0	86	0	71	0
Home economics	48	28	40	54	14	91	41	36	43	49	36	13	50	31	48	41	19	0	33	0	52	14	48	29
Industrial arts	46	29	42	52	14	90	39	34	41	47	36	13	46	32	47	44	14	5	24	5	43	14	43	19
Art	56	36	35	58	11	86	50	41	37	57	62	21	48	38	42	45	66	5	66	5	62	19	43	29
Crafts	12	22	10	36	5	50	10	25	10	30	12	14	13	21	11	21	10	5	5	5	5	14	0	14
General music	53	24	29	25	8	28	46	22	29	21	62	15	51	20	32	24	62	5	66	5	52	10	38	10
Vocal music	12	46	8	57	7	65	13	39	10	43	18	24	20	72	12	40	29	10	19	10	24	14	5	10
Instrumental music	12	77	9	83	7	92	15	86	13	86	14	74	21	90	13	89	0	43	5	66	24	76	10	76
Orchestra	0	49	0	51	4	58	0	44	0	46	0	28	0	34	0	33	0	5	0	10	5	10	0	10
Foreign language	6	37	10	53	10	82	9	42	10	50	11	12	7	36	8	42	0	5	0	10	5	10	0	10
Typing	7	13	7	31	5	56	5	13	6	21	0	5	9	12	8	21	0	5	5	5	0	5	10	5
Speech	5	15	5	24	7	40	7	16	3	25	11	6	12	19	12	22	5	0	5	0	10	5	0	10
Drama	0	15	1	29	2	42	0	26	3	34	0	15	0	26	5	32	0	10	0	5	5	10	1	10
Photography	0	9	0	15	2	25	0	13	0	16	0	10	0	15	0	18	0	5	0	5	0	10	0	5
Career education	14	10	17	11	19	24	31	12	32	15	19	4	39	7	40	10	19	0	24	0	52	0	33	0
Spelling	54	1	49	3	38	1	72	3	68	3	87	0	71	0	62	0	100	0	100	0	81	0	67	0
Chorus	0	59	0	69	6	83	0	63	0	71	0	40	0	59	0	67	0	10	0	15	0	38	0	38

R = Required, E = Elective

145

TABLE 118A
Scope of Ability Grouping by Population

	City of 150,000+	Suburban	25,000-149,999	5,000-24,999	Rural
Grouping—All grades All subjects	9	6	9	14	12
Grouping—All grades Certain subjects	76	69	68	65	59
Grouping—Certain grades All subjects	1	1	2	0	5
Grouping—Certain grades Certain subjects	13	16	15	19	22
Different grouping system	1	8	6	2	2

TABLE 118B
Scope of Ability Grouping by Enrollment

	<400	400-599	600-799	800-999	1,000-1,399	1,400+
Grouping—All grades All subjects	14	10	7	11	9	7
Grouping—All grades Certain subjects	62	63	68	66	77	86
Grouping—Certain grades All subjects	4	3	1	0	0	0
Grouping—Certain grades Certain subjects	20	20	18	17	8	7
Different grouping system	0	4	6	6	6	0

TABLE 122A
Criteria for Admittance to Gifted Programs by Per-Pupil Expenditure

	<$1,200	$1,200-1,799	$1,800+
No progam	32	32	29
Have program	68	68	71
Criteria			
Grades (GPA)	34	41	46
Student interest	24	30	45
Teacher recommendation	68	74	83
Standardized tests	76	80	85
Other	15	18	24

TABLE 125A
Funded Programs by Population

	City of 150,000+	Suburban	25,000-149,999	5,000-24,999	Rural
No federal or state funding	2	3	3	1	0
Funded programs	98	97	97	99	100
Types of Programs					
Federal Title I (ESEA)	57	56	51	69	83
State Compensatory Education	28	19	27	20	20
Vocational Education	40	35	43	40	31
Impact Aid	35	16	23	20	15
Career Education	42	32	30	34	31
Special Education	83	70	79	77	78
Bilingual Education	47	22	29	15	13
Assistance to Indochinese Refugee Children	12	5	14	5	2
Desegregation	40	6	5	2	1
Title IV—ESAA (Instructional)	55	60	57	70	73
Title III or IV C (Innovative Programs)	22	24	24	22	24
Other	6	6	6	5	5

TABLE 126A
Interscholastic Sports for Boys by Population

	City of 150,000+	Suburban	25,000-149,999	5,000-24,999	Rural
No interscholastic	12	7	9	3	6
Have interscholastic	88	93	91	97	94
Football	19	25	33	30	30
Basketball	31	37	41	44	40
Baseball	12	16	14	10	11
Softball	7	4	5	2	4
Track	28	35	38	36	32
Wrestling	12	27	23	20	18
Swimming	7	7	9	6	3
Gymnastics	9	9	8	4	2
Tennis	10	10	4	11	3
Volleyball	7	6	4	2	3
Soccer	11	14	9	6	6
Ice hockey	<1	2	2	2	<

TABLE 127A
Interscholastic Sports for Girls by Population

	City of 150,000+	Suburban	25,000-149,999	5,000-24,999	Rural
No interscholastic	9	7	8	4	6
Have interscholastic	91	93	92	96	94
Football	<1	1	2	1	<1
Basketball	26	35	39	36	37
Baseball	2	1	2	<1	<1
Softball	14	19	17	11	15
Track	28	35	37	35	31
Wrestling	1	1	2	2	0
Swimming	7	8	9	5	2
Gymnastics	13	16	13	9	3
Tennis	11	11	13	22	4
Volleyball	21	27	29	33	21
Soccer	8	9	6	4	4
Ice hockey	1	<1	<1	<1	0

TABLE 132A
Data Processing by Enrollment

	<400	400-599	600-799	800-999	1,000-1,399	1,400+
No	85	41	33	18	22	31
Yes—Scheduling	13	48	56	75	69	63
Yes—Recordkeeping	6	35	46	58	58	50
Yes—Report card	9	47	51	70	69	56

TABLE 132B
Data Processing by Per-Pupil Expenditure

	<$1,200	$1,200-1,799	$1,800+
No	49	37	31
Yes—Scheduling	43	54	61
Yes—Recordkeeping	33	43	46
Yes—Report card	41	48	59

TABLE 134A
Opinions About Ability Grouping Policies by Enrollment

	<400	400-599	600-799	800-999	1,000-1,399	1,400+
Grouping in all grades and in all subjects	18	7	10	13	5	8
Grouping in all grades and in certain subjects	48	60	59	59	68	75
Grouping in certain subjects and in all grade levels	4	2	1	0	1	0
Grouping in certain grade levels and in certain subjects	16	21	17	19	8	13
Should be a system different from alternatives listed	5	2	6	4	6	0
Should be no ability grouping	9	8	7	5	12	4

TABLE 135A
Opinions About the Role of Special Education in Middle Schools by Grade Level Organization

	Total	7-8-9	7-8	6-7-8	5-6-7-8	Other
Integral part of entire program (Mainstreaming)	68	63	73	68	57	80
Important supplemental program for selected students	31	34	26	30	43	20
Unnecessary or inappropriate	1	3	1	2	0	0

TABLE 143A
Opinions About the Ideal Middle Level Grade Organizational Structure by Population

	City of 150,000+	Suburban	25,000-149,999	5,000-24,999	Rural
7-8-9	28	14	20	14	16
7-8	12	17	19	24	18
6-7-8	50	58	54	51	51
5-6-7-8	7	6	3	3	9
Other	10	5	4	8	6

TABLE 143B
Opinions Regarding the Ideal Middle Level Grade Organizational Structure by Enrollment

	<400	400-599	600-799	800-999	1,000-1,399	1,400+
7-8-9	18	13	15	25	25	20
7-8	18	18	17	15	26	13
6-7-8	42	59	59	49	43	60
5-6-7-8	15	3	2	5	4	6
Other	7	7	7	6	2	1

TABLE 146A
Opinions About Optimal Number of Students for a Middle Level School by Population

	City of 150,000+	Suburban	25,000-149,999	5,000-24,999	Rural
<400	5	2	2	7	35
400-599	11	19	22	38	40
600-799	36	43	51	35	18
800-999	28	25	18	12	6
1,000-1,399	14	11	7	8	1
1,400+	6	0	0	0	0

TABLE 151A
Opinions Regarding Support for Administrative Tenure by Population

	City of 150,000+	Suburban	25,000-149,999	5,000-24,999	Rural
Yes	81	63	62	61	62
No	19	27	38	39	38

TABLE 151B
Opinions Regarding Support for Administrative Tenure by Enrollment

	<400	400-599	600-799	800-999	1,000-1,399	1,400+
Yes	55	62	66	69	79	58
No	45	38	34	31	21	42